The PASTOR *as* THEOLOGICAL STEWARD

Al Truesdale, Editor

THE FOUNDRY
PUBLISHING®

Cover design: Caines Design
Interior design: Sharon Page

Library of Congress Cataloging-in-Publication Data
A complete catalog record for this book is available from the Library of Congress.

The internet addresses, email addresses, and phone numbers in this book are accu-
rate at the time of publication. They are provided as a resource. The Foundry Publish-
ing® does not endorse them or vouch for their content or permanence.

10 9 8 7 6 5 4 3 2 1

"The Christian faith is the most exciting drama
that ever staggered the imagination of man—
and the [doctrine] is the drama."
—Dorothy Sayers, *Letters to a Diminished Church*

"Ordination is God's permission to speak and
act for that gospel which invented the church
and is not invented by the church."
—Robert Jenson, *Visible Words*

CONTENTS

CONTRIBUTORS

Deirdre R. Brower-Latz, PhD
Principal and Senior Lecturer in Pastoral and Social Theology
Nazarene Theological College
Manchester, United Kingdom

T. Scott Daniels, PhD
Senior Minister, Nampa College Church of the Nazarene
Pastoral Scholar in Residence, Northwest Nazarene University
Nampa, Idaho

Dean Flemming, PhD
Professor of New Testament and Missions
MidAmerica Nazarene University
Olathe, Kansas

Stephen G. Green, DMin
W. N. King Chair of Theological and Biblical Studies
Southern Nazarene University
Bethany, Oklahoma

Timothy M. Green, PhD
Dean, Millard Reed School of Theology and Christian Ministry
Professor, Old Testament Theology and Literature
Trevecca Nazarene University
Nashville, Tennessee

Steven Hoskins, PhD
Associate Professor of Religion
Trevecca Nazarene University
Nashville, Tennessee

Diane Leclerc, PhD
Professor of Historical Theology
Northwest Nazarene University
Nampa, Idaho

Jesse C. Middendorf, DMin
General Superintendent Emeritus, Church of the Nazarene
Executive Director of the Center for Pastoral Leadership
Nazarene Theological Seminary
Kansas City, Missouri

Mark R. Quanstrom, PhD
Senior Pastor, College Church of the Nazarene
Bourbonnais, Illinois
Director of the Center for Theological Leadership
Northern Seminary
Lisle, Illinois

Jeren Rowell, EdD
President, Nazarene Theological Seminary
Professor of Pastoral Ministry
Kansas City, Missouri

C. Jeanne Serrão, PhD
Professor of Biblical literature
Mount Vernon Nazarene University
Mount Vernon, Ohio

Al Truesdale, PhD
Emeritus Professor of Philosophy of Religion and Christian Ethics
Nazarene Theological Seminary
Kansas City, Missouri

Samuel Carl W. Vassel, DMin
District Superintendent
Metro New York District Church of the Nazarene
Valley Stream, New York

INTRODUCTION

ELDERLY MRS. FOUSHEE showed up one Sunday wearing her characteristic smile and carrying a large wreath made of plastic bags. We had recently renovated our sanctuary, and Mrs. Foushee wanted to make her contribution. "Pastor," she said, "I want you to place this on the wall behind the pulpit."

In my first assignment as a pastor, I was as green as a person could be. I had been taught sermon construction, systematic theology, and other things required for Christian ministry. But I had not been taught what to do with a large wreath composed of dry-cleaner bags lovingly intended for a sanctuary.

I had just been introduced to the world of competing loyalties all Christian ministers face, the always-present tension between comforting and discomforting the people of God. Theology was about to become "practical."

When Paul assigned Titus—his "true son in our common faith" (Titus 1:4)—to Crete, he identified numerous parts of his charge. Titus's stewardship included taking corrective and disciplinary measures (1:5, 10-16; 3:14). He had important administrative responsibilities to discharge (1:6-9). Paul counseled Titus on exemplary clergy conduct (3:9). But uniting all dimensions of ministry, Paul counseled Titus to "teach what is consistent with sound doctrine" (2:1, NRSV). To fulfill his charge, Titus must principally be a steward of the gospel of God. Other parts of his assignment were urgent and important. They would require cultivating Christian community (*koinonia*). However, to be truly Christian, all facets of ministry would require a uniting theological commission and center. Paul issued an identical charge to Timothy: "Watch your life and doctrine closely. Persevere in them, because if you do, you will save both yourself and your hearers" (1 Tim. 4:16).

Responsibilities of a parish minister seem endless. Wisdom and energies are taxed from every direction. He or she must work to balance church budgets, oversee staff assignments, provide for the education of his or her children, engage the wider community, satisfy denominational requirements, and sometimes negotiate disagreements among church members. All of these are important and must be attended with care. But the temptation is to confuse "the urgent" with one's primary calling to "contend for the faith that was once for all entrusted to God's holy people [saints]" (Jude v. 3).

If ever a minister experienced competing responsibilities it was the apostle Paul. A survey of the problems the church in Corinth presented can prove that. He lived in anguish over the failure of his fellow Jews to embrace the gospel (Rom. 9:1-5). He repeatedly confronted claimants who contested the gospel he preached, threatening, in one instance, to destroy the foundations he had laid in Galatia and, in other instances, hounding him from one city to another. Paul also wrestled with finances, having to raise funds for himself and for poor Christians in Jerusalem.

But Paul never wavered from the primary reason for which Christ had called him. He embraced the principal standard by which his Lord would judge him. Having his ministry "through God's mercy" (2 Cor. 4:1), he had been "set apart for the gospel of God" (Rom. 1:1). Christ had sent him to "preach the gospel—not with wisdom and eloquence, lest the cross of Christ be emptied of its power" (1 Cor. 1:17). He was a steward of "the mysteries of God" (4:1, RSV), a servant of the gospel (Col. 1:23). He refused to use his impressive education to convince people through cunning. Whatever gain he had acquired as a star pupil in Jerusalem, a rising pride of the Pharisees, a Hebrew of the Hebrews, and an envied Roman citizen, he now considered rubbish for the "surpassing worth of knowing Christ Jesus [his] Lord" (Phil. 3:8). Above all, Paul must "gain Christ and be found in him, not having a righteousness of [his] own, based on the law, but that which is through faith in Christ" (vv. 8-9, RSV). Refusing to tamper with God's word, Paul trusted the word of God and respected each person's conscience (2 Cor. 4:1-2).

Ministry contexts differ. In some parts of the world, Christian pastors and their congregations are confronted by outright hostile opposition. In other places, they are confronted by an increasingly aggressive secularism that schemes to chase the church from the public square and to reduce the Christian faith to history's dustbin, to mere subjective sentiment. Many pastors battle idolatrous consumerism, galloping individualism, and currents of fragmentation that tear at *koinonia*. Others confront spirit-draining poverty and political oppression. Orthodox clergy everywhere confront challenges to biblical moral norms inside (2 Pet. 2:1-3) and outside the church. In many ways, we can now more easily identify with the early Christian fathers, buffeted by heresy within the church and opposition from the Roman Empire.

Whatever their parish contexts, in the words of French Roman Catholic philosopher Chantal Delsol, all pastors contend with bogus forms of Christianity fashioned in the image of their creators, characterized by doctrines alien to orthodox Christian tradition, and far removed from historical grounding. The counterfeits are "invented by the first 'prophet' who happens to come along."[1]

Contributors in this book write in the spirit of John Wesley, whom today's Wesley scholars believe is best described as a practical theologian. Wesleyan theologian Randy Maddox says that at the most basic level, for Wesley, theology "comprised the (often implicit) convictions and depositions that frame believers' lives in the world." The practical theologian is committed to nurturing "authentic Christian convictions and dispositions in believers" as a communal activity in which "responsible grace" can thrive.[2] Practical theology should be holistic (engaged with doctrine, discipleship, and character), contextual, and transformative. It is marked by "a disciplined concern to form and norm the Christian worldview in believers."[3] In that spirit, as Stephen Green says in his chapter, this book "is meant for the people of God" and for the pastors who shepherd them.

The Pastor as Theological Steward serves that goal. Its purpose is to aid pastors, whatever their context, as they embrace and practice the standards for theological stewardship commended by Jesus and the apostles and as championed through the centuries by apostolic Christian faith. The book is energized by hope that it will be used of the Holy Spirit to encourage and equip stewards of the mysteries of God (Rom. 16:25; Eph. 1:9; 3:9; Col. 1:26; 2:2; 4:3; 1 Tim. 3:16), who are responsible for nurturing congregations in Christian faith and practice.

The contributors have expertise in their respective facets of theological stewardship. Equally important, they have a keen appreciation for the challenges pastors face. They are passionate about assisting parish clergy and come as colleagues, as "fellow elder[s]" (1 Pet. 5:1), in support of "shepherds of God's flock" (v. 2). The contributors "pull up a chair" beside pastors and pray the Holy Spirit will *fan the flame of the gift of God within us* (2 Tim. 1:6).

Soli Deo gloria.

1

STEWARD OF THE GOSPEL OF GOD

T. Scott Daniels, PhD

We speak as those approved by God to be entrusted with the gospel.
We are not trying to please people but God, who tests our hearts.

—1 Thessalonians 2:4

IT TOOK ME more time than I expected to finish my doctoral dissertation in theology and ethics. When it was finally complete and defended, my wife threw a party to celebrate. During the festivities, I overheard our oldest son, who was seven years old at the time, talking to one of his friends who asked, "Caleb, why is your family throwing this party?" He responded, "We're celebrating because my dad is finally a doctor now. But he's not the kind that can help anyone."

In my most anxious moments, I have often feared Caleb's statement was not only inadvertently funny but also accidentally prophetic. Although I find the professional discipline of theological ethics fascinating, I am not sure how helpful or relevant it is in the everyday life of people.

Unfortunately, I can confess to having the same anxieties connected to my role as a pastor. If any vocation could be helpful, it should be the occupation of the pastor. However, in today's world, the work of clergy can feel increasingly irrelevant for everyday life. All of us in ministry read studies and analyze statistics about the culture's increased secularity, the decline in church attendance, and people's growing suspicion of the institutional church. There are days when I feel as if I'm fighting for the future of my chosen vocation.

I accepted the call to ministry out of obedience and because I wanted to help others. However, I'm not always confident people outside of the church, and sometimes even inside, are looking to me for help. And so, I'm tempted to forsake the unique role of pastoral ministry in an increasing quest for relevance. What are the forces that tempt us to give up our unique calling?

Temptations in the Wilderness

Each Synoptic Gospel writer gives us an account of the temptations of Jesus. After passing through the waters of baptism, and receiving the anointing of the Holy Spirit, like a freshly ordained minister headed out into the world to be a blessing in the lives of others, Jesus launches the proclamation of the kingdom by first being drawn into the emptiness of the wilderness. The wilderness is intentionally a place of deficit. It is the place where we fear there will be no provision, no goodness, no beauty, and no meaningfulness in life. In the exodus narrative, the wilderness is the place of formation for God's people to become the unique light to the nations, embodying the way of God in the world. It is not enough for God to take Israel out of Egypt; God must take Egypt out of them. Like a spiritual boot camp, the wilderness is where God removes the imagination and formation of Egypt out of his people Israel. It's no wonder that in the life and ministry of Jesus, the advent of the new creation must begin also by experiencing the formation that can occur only in the vacuum of exile in the wilderness.

As Jesus recapitulates or reembodies the story of Israel, he passes through the waters to confront three great tests. Satan does not tempt Jesus to define the kingdom of God in ways that are obviously evil. Rather, the temptations are subtle forms of perceived helpfulness and relevance.

In the first temptation, Satan invites the famished Jesus to use his power to turn stones into bread. The devil implores Jesus to do something that seems inherently good. Jesus has the power to take the material reality of creation and use it as a commodity to meet people's needs, satisfy their appetites, and fulfill their innate desires. What could possibly be wrong with supplying bread for the needy? Didn't Yahweh supply manna to his hungry people in the wilderness?

The subtle but very real temptation for Jesus, and for us, is to use the gifts of the Spirit primarily to satisfy desire rather than to transform the heart. As Eugene Peterson states, "It is the temptation to deal with myself and others first and foremost as consumers. It is the temptation to define life in consumer terms and then devise plans and programs to accomplish them 'in Jesus' name.'"[1] It is not that needs like these are unimportant. It is obviously important for people to eat, to live, and to have the basic needs of life supplied. The problem, however, is when our desire to help meet the world's physical needs reduces ministry to satisfying appetites that are, in the end, insatiable. We need bread to live, but the life of the kingdom is not found in bread alone. And the role of the minister cannot be fulfilled by the quest for meeting and ending physical needs.

In the second temptation, the devil coaxes Jesus to throw himself off the highest point of the temple, requiring all the hosts of heaven to rescue him in a display of power. In the early days of Jesus's ministry, relatively few were following. Nothing would have gained the attention and adoration of a crowd (in the center of Jewish religious life) faster than a massive display of signs and wonders.

Years ago, I was in a two-week seminar taught by a well-known expert in church growth. There were a couple of hundred ministry students in the course along with me. We were all young and hopeful that we could go out into pastoral ministry and grow a large church and achieve various degrees of ecclesial success. The course covered many important insights, some I still use to this day. However, on the last day of the course the professor devoted the lecture to the three or four key methodologies known to cause congregations to grow rapidly. I couldn't help but notice that they were all performance-driven methodologies designed to be highly attractional and attention grabbing. In fact, the final statement from the professor was, "If you really want to grow a church [and we all leaned in closely because we all really wanted to grow a church], you will focus your ministry on displays of signs and wonders."

I remember sitting there with a couple of my friends in stunned silence. The idea was not surprising. All one needs to do is flip through the channels to find large arenas filled with people drawn to the power of religious healers. What seemed so odd and shocking was that this church growth expert's motivation for participating in signs and wonders of the Spirit was not because that is what the Bible invites the church to live into or where the Spirit seems to be uniquely moving in this historical moment. It was not even because our theology invites us to find God actively at work in the miraculous. Rather, we were transparently being encouraged to engage in the miraculous work of God to gain a following, grow a crowd, and fill the pews.

Once again, like filling hungry stomachs, healing bodies is obviously not bad. Healing people through the miraculous presence of the Holy Spirit is a vital part of Jesus's ministry, a clear sign the new creation is breaking into the world through him. Nevertheless, as it was for Jesus, our temptation is to reduce ministry to demonstrations of power that excite the imaginations of the curious.

Although the miraculous draws the attention of the multitudes, the constant pressure in our day to perform and feed the experiential emotions of the faithful puts incredible stress on ministers and their staff. Week after week, they are tempted to ascend the highest points of the experiential temple and throw themselves down for the awe and attention of others.

The devil's third temptation is related to power. If Jesus will simply bow down and orient himself toward the world in the impersonal and non-sacrificial ways practiced by the principalities and powers, then all authority and control will be given to him. There is a rule in relationships that the one who is willing to withhold love has the most power. Worldly power usually flows through threats of coercion. That is why war, or even the threat of violence, is history's most frequent method for imposing our will upon others.

In my lifetime, one of the ways the American church has fought for cultural relevance is through increased political pressure. No longer willing to sit on the sidelines of power, the church in America, in recent decades, has used its significant influence to support policies, laws, and candidates willing to fight for its interests. Likewise, the church has been willing vocally and publicly to oppose—and even demonize—politicians and leaders whom it perceives as opponents. No doubt political involvement by Christians has accomplished much that is good. I would even argue that civic participation is part of our responsibility as those given dominion over creation. However, it seems increasingly clear that the church's willingness to enter the ring of political battle, and the way it has used power to fight various "culture wars," has greatly diminished its Christian witness and caused many in our culture to view the church as just one more political interest group.

Jesus refused to be isolated from the problems of the world. However, he resisted the temptation to seize the impersonal posture of coercive power to rule and regulate the world, though that posture may be effective for gaining control over others. Instead, Jesus was faithful to the unique cruciform way of the kingdom.

President Theodore Roosevelt may have been correct—the best way to exert control in the world may be to "talk softly and carry a big stick." Nevertheless, the distinct political posture of the kingdom is to take up the cross and follow Jesus.

I want to emphasize again that the temptations Jesus faced in the wilderness were not evil on face value. It is not an inherently bad thing to feed people, to draw them to the healing beauty of Christian faith, or even to rule the world justly and efficiently. The problem is that these emphases are secondary to the primary purpose of the kingdom. They distract us from what is essential in the ministry of Jesus, and they too often put the church in positions contrary to the cross. As ministers these temptations threaten to move us from our primary calling as stewards of the gospel and to make us guardians of things secondary to our core mission.

So, what is the central vocation of the minister? What is the primary vocation Jesus embraced in the wilderness by resisting the temptation to make other seemingly good things central?

Early in the Gospel of Mark, as Jesus was gathering his disciples, and the signs of the kingdom of God were clearly visible in exorcisms and miracles, a large crowd gathered at the door, waiting for more miracles. But early in the morning, Jesus snuck away to a deserted place. Naturally, the confused disciples found him and exclaimed, "'Everyone is looking for you!' Jesus replied, 'Let us go somewhere else—to the nearby villages—so I can preach there also. *That is why I have come'"* (Mark 1:37-38; emphasis added). Here again, Jesus resists the temptation to define his ministry solely as healing and deliverance. As important as those signs of the kingdom are, preaching or proclaiming the good news of the kingdom took priority.

Guardians of the Gospel

The original meaning of the English word "gospel" is simply "good news." Christian faith in its most basic form is the proclamation of good news to the world. N. T. Wright has suggested that all good news, and in particular the good news central to the Christian gospel, has three aspects. *First*, good news always comes within a larger context. It does not happen in a historical vacuum. It is announced in response to and within a much larger story. *Second*, good news announces that something has happened within the reality of history that now makes a difference. The news is good because it changes how things are going to be. *Third*, good news introduces a new period of waiting and expectation. To summarize, people have received good news when some event has changed the trajectory of events. Now, in joyful response, they can adjust their lives and expectations accordingly. "What good news regularly does, then, is to put a new event into an old story, point to a wonderful future hitherto out of reach, and so introduce a new period in which, instead of living a hopeless life, people are now waiting with excitement for what they know is on the way."[2]

In the New Testament context, the word "gospel" when applied to the life, death, and resurrection of Jesus was likely borrowed from its use among the turbulent events that often occurred within the shifting powers of the Roman Empire. In 31 BCE, when Octavian defeated Antony, ending thirteen years of civil war, *good news* certainly would have gone through the empire that Octavian—soon to be made Caesar Augustus—had won the decisive battle at Actium, thus bringing peace, security, and prosperity to the Roman world. In the context of the empire's civil war, this event was proclaimed as *gospel*, as the good news, that the war was over, and Octavian's victory had now initiated a new era of hope and expectation for the people.

In a quick survey of New Testament texts, I counted over one hundred uses of the word "gospel" or "good news" to describe not only what Jesus proclaimed as his primary message but also what the apostles in the early church described as their primary mission and message. The list expands even further if references to "the message," "the word of God," "the mystery of Christ," "truths of faith," "the truth," or other similar descriptions of the gospel are included. Repeatedly, especially in Acts and the Epistles, early church leaders described their primary purpose and calling as being servants or stewards of this gospel—this good news. "This, then, is how you ought to regard us: as servants of Christ and *as those entrusted* with the mysteries God has revealed" (1 Cor. 4:1; emphasis mine). Like Jesus, the apostles may have cared for the needy, performed miracles, or confronted civic leaders. But they saw themselves first and foremost as entrusted with stewardship of the gospel.

I am sure that if each of us, as ministers, was asked to write out or formulate the message of the gospel, no two versions would be the same. For example, here are four recent articulations or summaries of the gospel by contemporary thinkers:

Tim Keller

The "gospel" is the good news that through Christ the power of God's Kingdom has entered history to renew the whole world. When we believe and rely on Jesus' work and record (rather than ours) for our relationship to God, that Kingdom power comes upon us and begins to work through us.[3]

Andy Crouch

The gospel is the proclamation of Jesus, in [two] senses. It is the proclamation *announced* by Jesus—the arrival of God's realm of possibility (his "kingdom") in the midst of human structures of possibility. But it is also the proclamation *about* Jesus—the good news that in dying and rising, Jesus has made the kingdom he proclaimed available to us.[4]

Scot McKnight

God loves you and everyone else and has a plan for us: the Kingdom community. But you and everyone else have a sin problem that separates you and everyone else from God, from yourselves, from one another, and from the good world God made for you. The good news is that Jesus lived for you, died for you, was raised for you, and sent the Spirit for you—so you all can live as the beloved community. If you enter into Jesus' story, by repentance and faith, you can be reconnected to God, to yourself, to others, into this world. Those who are reconnected like this will live now as God's community and will find themselves eternally in union with God and communing with others. Those who preach this gospel will not deconstruct the church. Instead, they will participate in what God is doing: constructing the Kingdom community even now.[5]

N. T. Wright

The gospel is the royal announcement that the crucified and risen Jesus, who died for our sins and rose again according to the Scriptures, has been enthroned as the true Lord of the world. When this gospel is preached, God calls people to salvation, out of sheer grace, leading them to repentance and faith in Jesus Christ as the risen Lord.[6]

Although varying to some degree, each author's definition of the Christian gospel evidences N. T. Wright's three-part movement of the gospel outlined earlier. The gospel is first rooted in a larger context—the ongoing story of redemption initiated in the activity of God in the Old Testament Scriptures and carried forward in the incarnation and ministry of Jesus. This story of redemption is necessary because the people of the world are divided from the purposes of the Creator and thus divided from one another and from the proper dominion and care of creation. "Sin"—in its personal, relational, and systemic manifestations—is the word often used to describe the broken, violent, and divided state in which we find the people and nations of the world.

Likewise, each of the four definitions agrees that something transformational in the life, death, and resurrection of Jesus has taken place that initiates a new possibility for people and for the world. Estrangement from God and violence toward one another need not be the last word. Different words such as "forgiveness," "reconciliation," and "holiness" (or "wholeness") are proclaimed as possibilities because of the new creation initiated amid the old one through the life, death, and resurrection of Christ.

This good news offers radical new possibilities for living. For each of the four authors the gospel is more than an intellectual affirmation; it is a very real and material possibility of a new existence, embodied in the life of the community of Christ followers and empowered by the Spirit to be a foretaste of the new creation.

Whatever else Christian ministers are, they are first and foremost women and men called to know, experience, proclaim, and embody the knowledge, hope, and possibilities of the gospel.

This has important implications for ministry preparation and for ongoing clergy formation. Those commissioned and ordained to be guardians of the gospel must know the story well. This entails deep devotion to and study of the primary source of this story, the Christian Scriptures. To know and love the story well is to understand and be able to rightly articulate how this story is woven through the various forms of literature that make up the Bible. Stewards of the gospel are stewards of the Scriptures.

Being stewards of the gospel implies not only knowing and understanding what has happened but also being formed by the prophetic imagination that makes the gospel good news in the present. Stewards of the gospel have learned how to proclaim the gospel's implications in ways that not only are persuasive but also capture and express its fullness, its hopefulness, and its universal possibilities. Preaching, unlike miraculous healing, is not a device for drawing a crowd. It is the church's divinely sanctioned means of grace for proclaiming a new creation into existence. Preaching is not a process for distributing new information but an opportunity to invite people into a new formation, a new creation.

And to live as stewards of the gospel, those leading the church should be prepared to understand, as much as possible, how to lead a community that gathers not only around the transforming Word but also around the incarnating Table of the Lord. Embodying the gospel in the day-to-day life of community is complex and challenging. It takes patience, humility, and the multiple gifts present in the body of Christ. However, this is the calling to which those who follow in the footsteps of the apostles have committed themselves.

Final Reflections

In his now classic ethics text, *After Virtue*, Alasdair MacIntyre warned that a culture that has lost its sense of purpose, or *telos*, would be drawn to the managerial, the therapeutic, and the experiential (what he calls the "rich aesthete"). The first time I read *After Virtue* I felt deeply convicted about my own sense of lostness and confusion about ministry. I heard MacIntyre as saying that when the church loses its primary sense of purpose, its ministers will be tempted to become managers, therapists, and creators of religious experience. These activities are closely related to the temptations of manipulative control, satisfying appetites, and grasping the displays of power offered to Jesus in the wilderness.

I immediately think about all of my sermon series that offer not the gospel but managerial techniques for life, such as Five Ways to Become a Better Parent, Three Biblical Principles for a Successful Life, and Six Core Truths for a Life of Significance. I am convicted by how easily the good news of new creation can be exchanged for offering people religious ways to manage their relationships, their finances, and their future.

I sense the tension within me because, as a pastor, I feel so inadequate as a counselor. Like so many, I feel increasing pressure to meet people's therapeutic needs in ways for which I am not fully equipped. And I struggle as I deal with people defining their spiritual well-being in direct proportion to their emotional needs.

I also realize how easy it is to get caught in the pressure to create, week after week, highly produced worship experiences for people who are being trained to be consumers of Jesus's "products" rather than to become disciples transformed by the present and coming new creation.

Like the temptations offered Jesus in the wilderness, none of these things are bad in themselves. In Christ there is wisdom for life, for peace deep within, and for emotional encounters with the transcendent and holy. However, these are by-products that flow from the gospel, not the good news itself. As pastors, we are first and foremost guardians of the mystery of faith: *Christ has died. Christ is risen. Christ will come again.*[7]

Recommended Resources

Noble, Thomas A. "Theology and the Wesleyan Tradition." 2021 MWRC Annual Lecture. YouTube video, 1:02:04. Posted by Manchester Wesley Research Centre, June 25, 2021. https://www.youtube.com/watch?v=DsBAThEqD98.

Peterson, Eugene H. *The Jesus Way: A Conversation on the Ways That Jesus Is the Way.* Grand Rapids: Eerdmans, 2007.

Root, Andrew. *The Congregation in a Secular Age: Keeping Sacred Time against the Speed of Modern Life.* Grand Rapids: Baker Academic, 2021.

———. *The Pastor in a Secular Age: Ministry to People Who No Longer Need a God.* Grand Rapids: Baker Academic, 2019.

Wright, N. T. *Simply Good News: Why the Gospel Is News and What Makes It Good.* New York: HarperOne, 2015.

2
STEWARD OF THE BODY OF CHRIST IN THE WORLD

Jeren Rowell, EdD

IT WAS ONE of the most meaningful and memorable things ever spoken to me. We were standing in the foyer of the church I had pastored for fourteen years. He was there to preach in the interim, and I was back for an official visit, now as district superintendent, not many weeks after my final Sunday as pastor. Having observed the vitality and love of the congregation, and having learned a bit about the vibrancy of their life together, he told me, "You did a good work here." Gathering my composure as he walked away, I nearly wept. I stood there reflecting on the meaning of my pastoral relationship with that congregation.

I do not know exactly what my friend had in mind, but I know how I received his words. I heard an affirmation of the Spirit deep in my soul, but not because of my abilities or hard work. The affirmation was about faithful stewardship, by God's grace, of that particular expression of the body of Christ in the world. I never thought of myself as a perfect pastor—far from it. But I did know my heart and life had been given to faithful pastoral care.

Good pastors carry about with them a constant guiding awareness of the sacred stewardship that is pastoral ministry. When a caring pastor is given charge of a local community of God's people, it is far more than a contractual agreement; it is a covenantal vow to steward well the holy communion of a Christian congregation. Faithful pastors do much more than accept a job assignment; they embrace what Paul told the Corinthians: "We have . . . opened wide our hearts to you" (2 Cor. 6:11). And Paul said this to a congregation not "easy" in any sense!

Sadly, too often the pastoral office is occupied by "technologists" or "pragmatists" who seem more committed to cultural markers of organizational success than they are to theologically grounded stewardship. The late Eugene Peterson shared more than thirty years ago his now well-known and oft-quoted lament:

> The pastors of America have metamorphosed into a company of shopkeepers, and the shops they keep are churches. They are

preoccupied with shopkeeper's concerns—how to keep the customers happy, how to lure customers away from competitors down the street, how to package the goods so that the customers will lay out more money.[1]

Unfortunately, the past thirty years have offered little to suggest that Peterson's assertion was misguided. The wholesale adoption of the contemporary leadership culture alongside an inadequate theological imagination has left many pastors languishing on the edges of what is really needed for faithful and effective congregational formation. The emphasis on marketing, organizational leadership, and attractional spectacle has left pastors burned out and God's people starved for something more than the latest conference theme or program.

The very idea of the church as a body (1 Cor. 12) signals that the church is much more than an institution or organization. The church is a living organism that must be cultivated, nurtured, and protected by those charged to "keep watch" (Acts 20:28) over the people of God. Further, the church as the body of Christ is not simply a voluntary organization comprising individuals who simply decide to join. Rather, the church is gathered by the Holy Spirit, whose breath (Ezek. 37; John 20) enlivens the embodied expression of Christ in the world to become "like living stones . . . being built into a spiritual house" (1 Pet. 2:5). When the guiding images of Christian community become more organic and less pragmatic, the role of pastor becomes more about familial nurture and less about organizational success.

The Body of Christ

In order to think well about pastoral life and practice, we must think well about the nature of the church. It seems that a ubiquitous critique of the "free church" or "believers' church" movement, which at least partly characterizes the American holiness movement, is the lack of a well-conceived and biblically grounded ecclesiology. A thorough treatment is beyond the scope of this chapter, but a few key observations may be consequential for a well-formed understanding of the pastor as steward of the body of Christ in the world.

The idea of the body of Christ is grounded in Scripture, for the Bible gives us the central narrative of God's initiating movement toward us in love. This "coming into the world" movement is encountered through God's incarnation in Jesus of Nazareth, revealed to us as the divine Son of God and Messiah (Christ). Jesus's birth, life, ministry, suffering, death, resurrection, and ascension constitute the embodied gospel—the church. No separation of the material and the spiritual, no gnostic diminishment of creatureliness in favor of disembodied deliverance from the world, is permitted. In Jesus Christ, bodies are sanctified, by the power of the Spirit, as vessels chosen for the *koinonia* (fellowship) that God intends to be expressed in God's good and beautiful creation. God's redemption from sin, the ministry of reconciliation, and the transformation into Christlikeness by the work of the Spirit are all of God. All this is "re-membered" at the Table of the Lord. Baptized into Christ's death and resurrection, Christians become the body of Christ, sent into the world to proclaim this restoring good news (Luke 24:30-35).

In the Bible, the phrase "body of Christ" typically refers to three things. *One* is the historical Jesus who lived and ministered in Palestine during the first century. A *second* reference is to the bread and cup of Communion or *Eucharist* (thanksgiving), as expressed in the Lord's words of institution, "This is my body. . . . This . . . is the new covenant in my blood" (22:19-20, RSV). How we understand the Communion elements as the presence of the risen Lord has been a subject of much debate. However, Wesleyans affirm that in the Lord's Supper, "Christ is present by the Spirit."[2]

A *third* way the phrase is used in the New Testament, as already noted, identifies the community of Christ followers—the church. As Ronald Rolheiser observes, "To say the word 'Christ' is to refer, at one and the same time, to Jesus, the Eucharist, and the community of faith."[3] What seems consequential about this in light of the present

31

discussion is recognizing the organic and dynamic nature of the body of Christ as embodied in the living, breathing people of God. Rolheiser adds that "Scripture, and Paul in particular, never tells us that the body of believers replaces Christ's body, nor that it represents Christ's body, nor even that it is Christ's mystical body. It says simply: 'We are Christ's body.'"[4] When this reality characterizes the clerical understanding of the church, it steers us away from perceptions of pastoral leadership that diminish the core pastoral ethos of love, protection, nourishment, guidance, and self-sacrificing service—all of which combine to define pastoral stewardship.

Theologically, the image of the church as the body of Christ points to the most essential theological formulation: the confession of God as three in one. From the perfect, holy communion of Father, Son, and Holy Spirit, the energy of divine love flows to summon all creation to "declare the glory of God" (Ps. 19:1). This holy fellowship is the love that sent the Son into the world to redeem it through the Spirit's power. This new creation (John 3:1-6; 2 Cor. 5:17), this deed of redemption, is first manifest in Jesus, who lived, died, and rose again. It is subsequently manifest in his body, which is the church, the redeemed (and being redeemed) people of God sent into the world to bear witness to this gospel. As Sam Powell puts it, "The creation of the church is the principal means by which God seeks to realize communion with humankind."[5] So it's no wonder that the life of this body of Christ would be placed under the care of those who by the Spirit are drawn from the community of faith, anointed, formed in the pattern of the Good Shepherd, and then by the Spirit sent back to the community of faith possessed of an almost maternal instinct to nurture God's precious gift. How terrible it would be, and how beside the point, to reduce the pastoral task to a concern for management, numerical growth, and "fleshly" success? Although leadership skills are clearly required, the central and motivating interest arises from a sacred obligation to steward God's wonderful gift with the same self-giving love that brought the church into existence.

Stewardship

Stewardship as a spiritual discipline echoes throughout Scripture. It is never self-serving or a means toward some material end. Stewardship of God's gifts is an act of worship and participation in God's work for the world. The foundational texts are the creation narratives of Genesis 1 and 2. In Genesis 1 we hear of the formation of the world, then the creation of humanity, and finally God's charge to "subdue" the earth, which carries no sense of utilitarian consumption, only God-ordained oversight. This is made clearer and more explicit in Genesis 2, where we hear God inviting Adam into the garden of Eden with the assignment "to work it and take care of it" (v. 15). Again, this is not simply a job description necessitated by a practical need to manage things; it finds its real force in the participatory identification with God, who is the ultimate caretaker and steward.

The call to stewardship weaves its way throughout the story of God. We see it in God's postflood covenant with Noah's family. We perceive it in God's forming, through Abram, a covenant people, who are given a covenant land and a covenant liturgy of worship. We observe it in the provision of priests, prophets, and kings for overseeing the community of faith and in the New Testament presence of apostles, bishops, and pastors commissioned to shepherd God's flock—the body of Christ in the world. So God's vision for thriving communities of faith entails stewardship, which at first reveals the very heart of God and is carried on through the Spirit. But stewardship is also embodied in those set apart to oversee the church's life and witness.

Understanding stewardship in this way has profound implications for conducting the pastoral office. If, in fact, we who are called to pastoral ministry are charged to steward the body of Christ in the world, then there are clearly things we *must* do, just as there are other things we *must not* do. Let's begin with what is prohibited and move toward what must be practiced. Pastors tuned to their identity as theological stewards know with crystalline clarity that ministry is never centered on them. We do not obey God's call in order to gain admiration, authority, or security. Failures in conducting the pastoral office are often rooted in a self-centered use of what is given by *grace* and intended as *gift* to others. Self-centered consumption is revealed in many ways, some of which are attitudes of entitlement, overly demanding expectations of others (especially one's family), the justification of selfish acts (e.g., gluttony, greed, lust), and treating the congregation as a means to one's own end. This usually causes failure to persist in one's assignment. At the heart of these characteristics is the failure to keep track of one's identity as "steward" and instead to begin thinking of oneself as "owner."

On the other hand, when pastors keep track of the *kenotic* (self-emptying) posture (Phil. 2:5-8) of Christlike ministry, they serve out of a life of prayer, which yields pastoral wisdom. Signs of a prayerful life are not only a capacity for a calm presence amid a fretful world but also an ability to "bring a word from elsewhere," as Walter Brueggemann puts it.[6] This is the poetic and imaginative speech that can call forth a faithful community that evidences the in-breaking kingdom of God in the world. When this is the *telos* (purpose or end) of ministry, then a pastor recognizes and accepts that Christian ministry is long-term work not achieved through shortsighted programs designed to "grow" church attendance or to increase a congregation's earthly "impact." Instead, it is achieved through an *eschatological* vision of the kingdom of God that grounds a congregation in its redeemed identity—a living sign of God's love for the world.

Can we see the profound implications of all this? Pastoral ministry can be rescued from thin notions of leadership, success, and spectacle and transformed into the deeply Christian virtues of patience, courage, and justice (or faith, hope, and love). Recovery of Christian virtues as the theological grounding of "pastor as steward" shapes ministers into a vocational identity marked by the person of Jesus, not by the "wisdom" of organizational leadership.

Pastoral Identity

The only way to steward the body of Christ well in the world is to have a clear understanding of pastoral identity. This means more than a pastoral job description or even denominationally assigned "duties of the pastor."[7] Pastoral identity finds its meaning in more than one's gifts. And it must arise from something more foundational than meeting the expectations or "felt needs" of people whom William Willimon described as people "of omnivorous desire."[8] Conducting pastoral ministry on the basis of meeting people's needs instead of God's desire for them is a recipe for exhaustion. Moreover, doing so can easily become idolatrous for pastor and people, for we are often tempted to identify our needs and desires contrary to God's will.

A healthy pastoral identity can find sufficient grounding only in the person of Jesus Christ. This is true not only of virtue and character shaped by grace and obedient response but also in the practices of ministry for which we have ample biblical resources from which to construct a faithful and effective model. The way of Jesus in the world was a way of contemplation and action (e.g., Matt. 14:13-23; Mark 1:32-35). His was a life of solitude and prayerfulness, but not of distance from the everyday stuff of life. The Jesus way was movement toward the people, especially those marginalized and seen as outcasts. This rhythm of contemplation and action is a proper way for pastors to construct their ministry in their congregation and community. The old advice was, "Spend the mornings in prayer and study, and spend the afternoons out among the people." While this counsel probably arises from a historical context that does not fit the complexities of contemporary ministry, the path of daily contemplation *and* action remains worthy of emulation.

From this way of viewing faithful stewardship of the pastoral office, we can also derive particular practices that serve to form the people of God as an authentic expression of the body of Christ in the world. The *first* of these is *presence*. It means being with parishioners in everyday life, whether critical or mundane. It involves showing up in a way that embodies God's movement toward us in love. It entails being willing not only to engage with people in the details of their lives but also to press the question, "How is it with your soul?" Yet pastoral presence can also be (and sometimes should be) wordless—the silent presence of being near as one who represents the presence of the Good Shepherd among God's flock.

Another essential practice for stewarding the body of Christ is the ministry of Word and Table. Because authentic pastoral care arises from the Word of God (first Jesus Christ and then the Scriptures) and the Sacraments, practices of the worshipping community are key components of faithful and effective pastoral care. There is perhaps no more important work of congregational stewardship than that of a pastor exegeting and proclaiming the Scriptures in service to God and congregants so that worshippers may hear a word from the Lord. When a pastor is able to stand, under the Spirit's authority, and faithfully proclaim the word, not only are individual Christians discipled, Christian communities are formed as hearers and doers of the word (James 1:22). As the written Word becomes a proclaimed and living word by the Spirit's power, congregants are called to respond to God's grace. A pastor's privilege is to set the "table of grace" at which believers not only remember the gift of God in Christ but are also "re-membered" (Rom. 12:4-5) as the body of Christ in the world. What could be a more essential and joyful act of pastoral stewardship?

Let's consider an often neglected pastoral practice—*stability*. The classical vows of ordination in the early church were vows of poverty, chastity, and obedience. In the sixth century, Benedict articulated a rule for his monastic community that included not only formational practices but also *stability* as a virtue to be developed. By stability Benedict meant a commitment to remain. This entails recognizing that we ministers of the gospel do not chart our own careers. We go where we are sent. While God's call is the genesis of vocational ministry, *sending*

36

is its direction or motion. In service to the gospel, the Holy Spirit *sends* ministers, through the work of the church, to faith communities. We would do well to remember that the Spirit's sending is never random or haphazard. It is always purposeful and stable. This means we dare not take matters into our own hands and leave an assignment simply because it has become difficult or because a more desirable opportunity arises. Stewarding the body of Christ in the world requires pastors willing to take the long view of discipleship and remain with those to whom they were sent, as long as God wills it.

For the World

Forming spiritually healthy congregations has as its purpose serving and advancing the gospel of God. While this should be assumed, experience tells us congregations can become self-serving, more interested in securing their own comfort and safety than in offering themselves as gifts to their neighborhoods and to the world. The church is "the hands and feet of Jesus" in the world, a statement attributed to Teresa of Ávila (1515-82). "Christ has no body now but yours, no hands but yours, no feet but yours. Yours are the eyes through which Christ's compassion must look out on the world. Yours are the feet with which He is to go about doing good. Yours are the hands with which He is to bless us now."[9]

While Teresa's words are not meant to replace our Lord, the exhortation is correct. The church is "the Body of Christ called together by the Holy Spirit through the Word."[10] It exists not for its own sake but "to express its life"[11] in worship and fellowship, but also in mission. Theologian Emil Brunner famously declared, "The church exists by mission as fire exists by burning."[12] The mission of Christ's church is not simply something we *do* to serve the Lord but the essence of who we *are* in the world. The body of Christ in the world serves God's mission to reconcile "the world to himself in Christ" (2 Cor. 5:19). The church fulfills its mission "by making disciples through evangelism, education, showing compassion, working for justice, and bearing witness to the kingdom of God."[13] Congregations of God's people conduct God's mission through unified purpose and organizational structure. This requires spiritual leadership not preoccupied with secondary interests but with focused identity and purpose and prayerful dependency upon the Holy Spirit. This explains why good pastoral leadership is so consequential for the church's mission in the world.

Doing a Good Work

When my friend said "You did a good work here," I think he meant to affirm and maybe even congratulate me for a good pastoral tenure. His words penetrated more deeply. In a flash of memory, years of ministry rushed through my mind—the joyful and painful times, occasions of victory and defeat. The "good work" affirmed in my soul was something no one else could notice. It was what I had signed on for in the first place. Paul's testimony was mine also. "I have been crucified with Christ and I no longer live, but Christ lives in me. The life I now live in the body, I live by faith in the Son of God, who loved me and gave himself for me" (Gal. 2:20).

Conclusion

By God's grace, a pastor as theological steward of the body of Christ in the world lives out Paul's commitment in alert awareness. To some, it might sound burdensome. But a Spirit-anointed pastor embraces the commitment with great grace and great joy! Thanks be to God.

Recommended Resources

Kreider, Alan. *The Patient Ferment of the Early Church*. Grand Rapids: Baker Academic, 2016.

Lathrop, Gordon W. *The Pastor: A Spirituality*. Minneapolis: Fortress Press, 2011.

Peterson, Eugene H. *The Pastor: A Memoir*. New York: HarperOne, 2011.

Purves, Andrew. *Reconstructing Pastoral Theology: A Christological Foundation*. Louisville, KY: Westminster John Knox Press, 2004.

——. *The Resurrection of Ministry: Serving in the Hope of the Risen Lord*. Downers Grove, IL: IVP Books, 2010.

Root, Andrew. *The Pastor in a Secular Age: Ministry to People Who No Longer Need a God*. Grand Rapids: Baker Academic, 2019.

Rowell, Jeren. *Thinking, Listening, Being: A Wesleyan Pastoral Theology*. Kansas City: Beacon Hill Press of Kansas City, 2014.

Willimon, William H. *Calling and Character: Virtues of the Ordained Life*. Nashville: Abingdon Press, 2000.

——. *Pastor: The Theology and Practice of Ordained Ministry*. Rev. ed. Nashville: Abingdon Press, 2016.

3
STEWARD OF THE SCRIPTURES

C. Jeanne Serrão, PhD

IT IS ESSENTIAL for a pastor to be a steward of the Scriptures. What he or she honors and discusses becomes important for his or her congregation. Modeling the correct use of the Scriptures in worship, conversations, Bible study, administration, and counseling has a formative impact upon congregants.

As stewards of the Scriptures, pastors must not only model correct usage and interpretation but also teach how to read and understand the Bible. Although pastors cannot conduct all the teaching, they must make sure all teachers and church leaders know how to read and interpret the Bible correctly. This chapter is designed to help pastors and congregations achieve this goal.

The Need

Each semester for the last twenty-two years, I have begun my introductory Bible classes with a "get acquainted" survey. I want to know the level of student acquaintance with the Bible. Most students come from Christian homes, several have participated in Bible quizzing, and over 50 percent have attended Sunday school for most of their lives.

What startles me is the lack of correlation between length of time attending church and Bible reading. This year, among ministry students, about one-third had read the Bible several times through; a third had read it through once, and a third, almost all the way through. The levels were lower for the general education Bible class, with 40 percent having read the Bible at least once and 60 percent having looked at the Bible occasionally. Over half of these checked "seldom" or "never."

This is not a new problem. Kenneth Berding, in his article "The Crisis of Biblical Illiteracy and What We Can Do about It," says the many distractions we live with—misplaced priorities and "unwarranted over-confidence"—answer the *why* question. He adds that studies show fewer than half the adults in the United States can name the four Gospels, 60 percent of Americans cannot name five of the Ten

Commandments, and 50 percent of graduating high school students think Sodom and Gomorrah were husband and wife.[1]

How can we as pastors be faithful stewards of the Bible in our churches? We have Bible studies, small groups, and preaching, but too often they do not seem to help people learn to read and understand the Bible for themselves. We agree that reading and understanding the Bible is vital for growth in Christlikeness.

Teaching Christians How to Read the Bible

We must intentionally teach people how to read the Bible. We can start as soon as a child learns to read and continue the instruction through children and youth programs. However, the situation is so dire that we must intentionally teach adults as well. The church seems to expect people to learn to read the Bible by listening to sermons or participating in Bible studies. But usually that does not happen. Moreover, because of today's distractions, people need to be motivated to read (more of this in the final section).

There is a perception that the Bible is difficult to understand. Therefore, someone else must interpret it for us. This was the practice during the Middle Ages, when most people were illiterate. However, today the problem has to do with the availability of numerous translations and the historical and cultural gap in understanding a book that was written over two thousand years ago in different cultures and languages.

Recognizing this as part of the problem, I took a lead from journalism and developed a simple method for reading and understanding the Bible that can be as detailed or as general as needed. It can be used with young children or in higher education. It consists of knowing the correct questions to ask. I apply to the study of Scripture what journalists call the "five Ws": *who, when, where, what,* and *why.* Answering the first three questions helps readers understand first-century writers and readers. Based upon the first three questions, the fourth and fifth questions prepare us to hear the text as it applies today. Proper Bible study requires *exegesis*, which means to "read out" the meaning of a biblical text. Many times the meaning of a text is straightforward. One needs only good translations. However, sometimes there is a danger that Scripture will be read out of context because we do not consider the historical and cultural settings.

The following questions provide a way to ask important questions about Scripture.

The *Who* Question

Who is writing and *who* is reading the passage in its original setting? Sometimes there is a second set of *who*s, as in narrative literature (e.g., the Gospels). In this case, we also want to know *who* is speaking and *who* is listening. Here, the two sets of *who* questions are central. In the Prophets and Epistles there are usually only two groups—the writers and/or prophets and the original readers.

We can answer the *who* question for young children after reading them a passage or Bible story. We begin exegesis with them by asking, "Who is talking and to whom are they speaking?" This trains children to notice these people as they hear Bible stories. The conversation can continue with questions such as, "Who is Jesus?" "Where was he born?" "Who were his mother and father?" and "Where did he grow up?" Depending on the age-group, teachers can clarify the meaning of the story or passage by adding historical and cultural contexts. For teens and adults, good resources can help them discover answers on their own and assist them in sharing those answers with others.

The appendix at the end of this book includes an example of an in-depth series of questions for an adult Bible study or teaching seminar. It requires research and access to modern commentaries with introductory sections that provide historical and cultural contexts.

Bruce Malina has written several books that help people understand cultural backgrounds. *The New Testament World: Insights from Cultural Anthropology* is well organized and helpful. For example, chapter 3 discusses "limited goods."[2] In the first century, everything from riches to health and children was believed to be limited. There was enough for everyone to have what he or she needed. However, some people had more than they needed, and so from this perspective, the rich had "stolen" from those without enough.

The epistle of James is critical of wealthy people (5:1-6). The apparent "hatred" of the rich seems extremely harsh to us. Why is James so condemnatory? The cultural perception of limited goods helps us understand. It is not so much about being wealthy as it is about failing to be generous, not taking care of those in need. A better translation of "rich" would be "greedy rich" to reflect the cultural understanding of limited goods. There is also a historical reason why James identifies with the poor and not the rich—but we will leave that to the next question.

The *When* Question

The *when* question is not so much concerned with specific dates as with events and their meaning for ancient people. What happened before the story impacts the language used and the hearers' understanding. Recently, my husband and I were talking about flying commercially. Immediately we thought about the security waiting lines. There are apps that tell how long security waits are for specific times and various airports. We tried to remember what it was like before the 9/11 attacks but found it difficult, even though we had often traveled domestically and internationally before 2001! The tragic events of 9/11 dramatically changed our travel context.

As with the *who* question, talk to young readers about the elements surrounding *when* an event happened. Show the immediate context by discussing what comes prior to the story. To increase understanding, talk about large historical events such as the oppression of Christians by the Romans. This teaches children to think about what else is happening during the time of a story. While children might not readily grasp the importance of history, they can understand how things that make people happy, sad, or angry affect how we talk to them or how they understand the world.

When studying with older teens and adults, use historical resources that address the period in the Mediterranean world. Often commentary introductions succinctly contain such information. Reading historical accounts and viewing historical videos can also help students put their feet in the shoes of first-century people (see the appendix for more guidance and resources).

Here is a brief illustration of how important cultural and historical contexts are for understanding Scripture. As Jesus and James made clear, the poor were very important for understanding the gospel and receiving God's kingdom (e.g., Matt. 19:21; Luke 6:20-21; 14:12-14). But why are they so often associated with righteousness? After Antiochus IV Epiphanes (d. 164 BC), a successor to Alexander the Great (356-323 BC), conquered Palestine, the religious elite and wealthy Jews, to ingratiate themselves with the new ruler, embraced the polytheistic Hellenistic culture. For three years, Antiochus exempted the Jews from paying taxes. But the poor did not benefit from the exemption. They were horrified by Hellenistic polytheism. Under the leadership of the orthodox Maccabees, who represented the poor, the Jews successfully rebelled and enjoyed eighty years of independence before the Roman conquest. The poor had opposed the pagans and refused to assimilate. Consequently, in the New Testament the poor are associated with the righteous.

The *Where* Question

This question examines the geographical context of speakers and listeners. How should this influence the understanding of a text's message? For example, why did Paul concentrate his missionary work on cities? Or why is water so important in the Bible? Names of cities and places are important because they provide insight into the physical context. They are important in part because they tell whether the setting is rural or urban, temperate or desert, and whether the place belonged to Jews in Palestine or in the Diaspora (Jews living outside Palestine). Asking *where* also provides insight into the animals mentioned, whether they are wild or domesticated. This is important when animals are used as metaphors.

Young readers can become aware of the biblical world by using digital satellite maps, globes, and videos. When studying a passage, show the location of the people. Help young readers learn to pronounce names of places. Preferably, by using a globe, children can touch and sense where they live and where ancient people lived. I heard a funny story about a child who grew up in Bethlehem, Pennsylvania. Because other towns in his area had biblical names, he thought Jesus was born in his town and ministered there.

While the comprehension of children is limited for some aspects of geography, teens and adults can appreciate geography more broadly. Like some people in the Bible, those who live in desert areas realize how important water is and learn to conserve it. After moving to central Ohio from arid Southern California, I was petrified by the huge bonfire a neighbor lit in his backyard. I feared my house would catch on fire. Why were there no yard sprinklers? The plentiful rain in Ohio (context) helps me appreciate geographical differences.

The appendix identifies resources for understanding and valuing first-century geographical contexts.

The *What* Question

This question lies at the heart of exegesis. Keeping in mind the first three questions, now we reread and begin the process of understanding what was said to the original audience. Many times the message is clear, but sometimes it needs to be heard in its original context. That requires keeping our feet in the context of first-century readers and listeners.

For young readers, the conversation turns to the text itself. Read a few sentences and then discuss what was read and what it meant to the original audience. Then read a few more sentences and repeat the process, thereby working through the whole story or passage. As appropriate, refer to the speaker and listeners and try to discern how they would hear the story or message.

Older teens and adults can look at the text more intensely: How did the author put the work together? What precedes and follows a passage? Stepping back to view the entire book or letter helps us see how a particular passage fits into the book as a whole. This offers insight but also narrows the interpretation because the meaning must fit into the overall purpose of a book.

A literary analysis of a passage is important for interpretation but can be intimidating. Do not engage in tedious detail about types of literature. Just stick to broad genres such as poetry, narrative, and history. Everyone can understand these basic types and their purposes. A poem generally deals with emotions, whereas history usually teaches. A narrative is a story, so examine the characters. How are they developed? What is the story's point?

Next follows an analysis of the text itself. Compare it in several translations. Note the differences. Depending on student level, using sources such as commentaries, ask, "Why are there differences?" Comparison also reveals key words or phrases. Then outline the main ideas and how the supplemental ideas fit (keep it simple). Finally, taking the main idea and its supplemental points, in your own words write what you believe to be the text's central thrust. This should help you understand the original message. The appendix contains an outline form of what we have just covered.

The *Why* Question

The answer to this question is why most people do an in-depth Bible study. They want to know what the passage means. To reach this point, we must ask a few other questions. Why did the speaker say what he or she said? What did he or she want the readers or hearers to do or understand? Are there cultural qualifiers that should be considered? Based on the answers, how does the original message translate into today's context?

Answering the *why* question requires synthesizing answers to the previous questions. Often when we understand the original meaning, the resultant meaning is obvious and applicable. However, when a text is difficult to understand (e.g., James 5:1-6), recall for example the distance between our modern perception of "unlimited goods" and the first century's perception of "limited goods." By recognizing cultural differences of this nature, we realize James is not talking about being rich but about having wealth without generosity. As employers, they hoarded, took advantage of, and oppressed their employees.

Another illustration helps make the point. In Romans 12:16, Paul instructs, "Do not be proud" and "Do not be conceited." He tells the Philippians, "Do nothing out of selfish ambition or vain conceit. Rather, in humility value others above yourselves" (Phil. 2:3). Paul warns against pride, and rightly so. Why did he do this? The first-century Greco-Roman culture was a culture of challenge. As the public face of their family, men were raised to seek honor. They challenged each other to increase their social standing. Often this happened through lawsuits. Such culturally conditioned pride often made unity in the church difficult. By contrast, Paul encouraged people to be humble, just as Christ humbled himself.

In our culture the challenge to being Christlike is not so much pride but low self-esteem. Encouraging humility for such people compounds their problem. The takeaway from this illustration is that in all instances we should learn to see ourselves as God sees us. This is good news for people with low self-esteem, especially as we learn from the Scriptures the gifts God has given us.

How to Read the Bible and Preach from Its Texts

As stewards of Scripture, pastors must teach congregants how to read the Bible by modeling proper reading in their sermons. While pastors should not "preach their homework," their preaching should let the congregation see how they read the Bible and reach their conclusions and applications. This is especially important when applications are made that are not obvious in the text. Understanding and explaining cultural contexts that differ from ours but which nevertheless yield valid applications for today are imperative.

The best way to help congregants grasp the importance of reading the Bible and reading it well is to read it in services of worship. This requires much more than reading a sermon text. Lectionary readings provide that larger context. Appointing others to share in publicly reading the lectionary lessons of the day is desirable. Prepared readers might even preface the reading by briefly applying one of the first three "Ws": *who, when,* or *where.* Then as a congregation's chief steward of the Scriptures, demonstrate how the sermon actually comes from the Scriptures that have been read.

Although there are diverse preaching styles, the use of narrative in preaching is a good way to model knowledge of the five Ws. Lenny Luchetti says the best way to get the attention of postmodern congregants is to tell a story—the Bible's story.[3] Storytelling appeals to the postlogical, postmodern mindset that requires being inspired before learning. Use of narrative in preaching emphasizes a text's setting, character development, and intention-getting problem(s). All of these arise from a text's context. Narrative demonstrates the importance and joy of in-depth Bible study.

Encourage Reading the Bible in Worship

In my introductory New Testament History and Literature class, I use group presentations based upon pagan, Jewish, and Christian festivals. In Jewish festivals, the story of Israel is rehearsed annually—for example, Passover, the story of the exodus, and Sukkot, the forty years of wandering in the desert. During these festivals Jews read biblical texts, some in unison. This happens every year, so that by adulthood Jews have memorized passages in Hebrew that tell their story.

The Christian story is told annually in congregations that use the lectionary and observe the Christian year. Annually reading and celebrating the Christian story should include reading in unison by the congregation, not just listening to readers at a lectern. Each year tell the story in different ways. Find creative ways for congregants to participate in reading and memorizing Scripture. Because information is so readily available, postmodernists often have poor memorization skills. We can help overcome that deficit through Bible stories and passages central to the Christian faith.

From the Jewish festivals, my students learn the combination of Bible reading and celebration. For example, each year a festival celebrates the end of Torah reading.[4] I suggest creating reading lists and each year celebrating those who complete their reading. Or do this monthly. For many years, in vacation Bible schools children have learned Scripture. We must find ways to do this for everyone.

Conclusion

I urge you as good stewards of Scripture to use the content of this chapter. Model good Bible reading in your preaching and counseling. Find creative ways to teach congregants how to read and embody the Scriptures. As you know, the situation is dire due to a lack of emphasis on reading and interpreting Scripture, but it can be done! Start with those who are open and willing to learn. Their success will influence others to learn. If the Word is truly a lamp to guide our way (Ps. 119:105), it is imperative that we incorporate ways to encourage people to read the Bible—and read it profitably.

Recommended Resources

Bird, Michael F. *Seven Things I Wish Christians Knew about the Bible*. Grand Rapids: Zondervan, 2021.

Boone, Dan. *Preaching the Story That Shapes Us*. Kansas City: Beacon Hill Press of Kansas City, 2008.

Malina, Bruce J. *The New Testament World*. 3rd ed. Louisville, KY: Westminster John Knox Press, 2001.

New Beacon Bible Commentary. 47 vols. Kansas City: Beacon Hill Press of Kansas City, 2008-21.

Shaped by Scripture Bible Study Series. Kansas City: Foundry, 2019-.

Truesdale, Al, ed. *Square Peg: Why Wesleyans Aren't Fundamentalists*. Kansas City: Beacon Hill Press of Kansas City, 2012.

Wright, N. T., and Michael F. Bird. *The New Testament in Its World*. Grand Rapids: Zondervan Academic, 2019.

4
STEWARD OF CHURCH HISTORY

Steven Hoskins, PhD

LET US AGREE that among the goals of each pastor is the desire to foster a thriving community of people marked by clear Christian identity. Believers join minds, hearts, and hands in remembering and being formed by all God accomplished in Christ.

Let us agree that pastor and people are part of the body of Christ, which has existed through the ages in every nation and culture.

Let us agree that by God's grace, as John Wesley taught, the people of God dispersed throughout the whole earth and through time constitute an uninterrupted witness to the gospel of Jesus Christ.

Let us agree that the history of that uninterrupted witness, which we call church history, is itself a means of grace. It unites us with Christian witness and faithfulness past and present. Church history bears dynamic testimony to the story of all God has done and continues to do among us. As the author of Hebrews reminds us (11:1–12:2), *remembering* well is an essential dimension of our faith. Obviously, *remembering* begins with what has already happened. Moreover, *remembering* well and *transmitting* it well is something we owe to our children and the future church. We are to transmit the long knowledge of God's redeeming work in the church and in the world. When correctly remembered, the stories of God's faithfulness are full of the Spirit's power for leading us into the future and imitating Christ and his saints (1 Cor. 11:1).

Stories and the Story

Each congregation has an important story, and so does each Christian. Theologian Wolfhart Pannenberg observes that the Christian faith is through and through a historical religion.[1] This entails that we are recipients and stewards of a goodly and rich heritage, "the faith which was once for all delivered to the saints" (Jude v. 3, RSV). The history of that faith begins with the story of Jesus the Christ. But it reaches back to the people of God in the Old Testament. It includes the early New Testament church. And it spans two thousand years of God's faithfulness and the church's witness. That history is replete with flesh and blood *witnesses* (Gk., *martyres*) to Jesus Christ. They served faithfully and died in the assignments where God had placed them.

As stewards of church history—stewards of God being with his church—the work of learning and retelling that story has been partly assigned to us as pastors. Through that story we lead congregations to know and bear witness to how God faithfully and creatively made us his own.

I learned this when in June 1990 I, as a fresh graduate of Nazarene Theological Seminary, first stepped into the pulpit of the Fulton Church of the Nazarene in Fulton, Kentucky. I was there for a tryout sermon. As I gazed at the people, I was immediately drawn to seven life-size faces in picture frames that hung in a perfectly aligned row on the rear wall of the church. Those faces formed the Fulton Nazarene hall of saints—that is, members recently deceased. Their pictures had been hung during the church's fiftieth anniversary. I quickly learned that the dead remain alive in the church as part of the communion of saints. Those pictures had names and stories to tell, stories that made the Fulton congregation who they were and who they were becoming.

Among them were Brother Howard, Sister Willie, and Tom. Brother Howard, a longtime attendee who refused to join the church because he did not believe in organized religion, had nevertheless paid expenses for evangelists and revivals so people could come to Christ. Sister Willie was the long-term mission society president, a person who raised her windows each night to pray for people in the hospital next door. On Wednesday evenings during prayer meeting, she read the missionary reading books aloud so everyone would learn the stories of sacrificial Christians around the world. That way, everyone could be counted when the "missionary reading book" statistics were reported to the Tennessee District at the end of the year. Tom was just Tom. He showed up every Saturday to clean the church, paint over the leaks in the ceiling, pray over each pew for the coming Sunday service, and put the (funeral-home) fans on the pews before the sanctuary was air-conditioned. Tom's photograph was included because he never accepted money for his work. Never! His was a holy calling whose value lay far beyond remuneration. Those saints are at the center of church history.

These Fulton stories can remind us that much of the work of ministry involves recounting the history bound up in memories of Christ's servants. Part of a pastor's responsibility is to keep memories alive and unite them with memories and stories of Christians in the church universal. The stewardship of church history entails accepting the responsibility to join the faith experiences and holy witness of local congregants with the faith once delivered to the saints universally.

What Church History Can Teach Us

As we practice pastoral stewardship, there are some things church history can teach us. *First,* we pastor the entire church: the living, the dead, and the broader community where God has placed us. Each congregation, each community of Christ's disciples living in their particular place, is a laboratory, a proving ground, for the whole of church history, because here Christ is redemptively at work, just as he has been for two thousand years. And here we as Christians are one with all those who have lived the faith before us. All of us, past and present, share a common faith in the Lord of the church. So stewarding church history means that as pastors we are students and transmitters of the long history of God with his people. This is a history that creates identity, helps shape discipleship, and infuses our stories with Christian meaning and values, goals and strategies. Fred Craddock, the eminent teacher of preaching, once told me in conversation, "If you can give people memories worth having, then the Holy Spirit will be at work and you will have done your work as a pastor."

Second, church history is not something "out there." It is unfolding in us as we live and tell our stories of faith. The character of Christ's church shapes our character and our worldview. We are taught just as those who have gone before us were taught. "Therefore," says the author of Hebrews, "since we are surrounded by so great a cloud of witnesses, let us also lay aside every weight . . . and run with perseverance the race that is set before us" (12:1, RSV). The stewardship of church history involves benefiting from language found in the ecumenical creeds, the historic Christian symbols, and the formative doctrines that constitute our common faith—without which we lose identity as Christians. This includes teaching congregations the story and language of faith as used in the New Testament. All of this is included in our baptism into Christ and the holy resurrection life that follows (Rom. 6:1-11; Eph. 5:25-27).

As Wesleyans, we understand the church and its history in an interesting, though not unique, way. On the one hand, we understand the church as a creative dynamic within a historical institution organically rooted in the Scriptures. Apostolic doctrines and the ecumenical creeds (tradition) are also essential for us. On the other hand, the church is the context in which we learn to experience God's grace in its fullness. This includes practicing the ancient means of grace through the sacraments, fellowship in the body of Christ, and holy living made possible by the saving and sanctifying presence of the Holy Spirit (see the discussion of *orthodoxy, orthopraxis,* and *orthopathy* in ch. 11).[2]

Third, by drawing from the well of church history in pastoral care we can find much in the "big pictures" of the past that can inspire and direct us today. This includes the rich examples of faithful witness in the first-century Jerusalem church, the eighteenth-century Evangelical Revival, and the growth of the church in Africa and China today. The big pictures include the stories of saints such as Phoebe in Romans 16, Susanna Wesley in England, and Susan Norris Fitkin in the Church of the Nazarene. Examples of the holy life—personal and communal—can be found in the *Didache,* the *Rule of Saint Benedict,* and the sixteenth-century Lutheran Moravian Communities. Inspiring examples of evangelism are seen in the monastic preaching of Anthony of Egypt (ca. 251–ca. 356) and the camp meetings and revivals of early twentieth-century America.

Fourth, not only does the stewardship of church history yield examples worth imitating, but it can also help us learn the skills of Christian responsibility and judgment. Errors by the church in the past can teach us not to make the same mistakes. Those errors can teach the consequences of taking Christ's church into our own hands for its control. These lessons can also teach the means for maturation in the faith.

Fifth, the church's history is a treasure house for rich prayers and effective sermons. From that treasure house we can draw instruction on Christian moral values—that is, how Christians have loved their neighbors as themselves and have ministered to the dispossessed. We become participants in that history by being reminded of the grand narrative of redemption and new creation. Not least, we learn that hope for Christ's church is secured by the certainty that the kingdom of God will be consummated as promised by our Lord.

The *sixth* and perhaps greatest value of the stewardship of church history lies in seeing how our churches and witness are part of the universal witness to Christ today and in seeing how to pray for the church, perhaps especially the persecuted church. Each Christian, each congregation, and each denomination that lives faithfully for the Lord of the church is part of that body about which the apostle Paul said, "Through the church the manifold wisdom of God [is being] made known to the principalities and powers in the heavenly places. This was according to the eternal purpose which [God] has realized in Christ Jesus our Lord" (Eph. 3:10-11, RSV). All Christians are our "traveling companions on the journey towards a kingdom whose prince has [gone] ahead and promised to escort us on the way."[3] Pastors as stewards of church history are privileged to help congregants realize they are part of the joyous and wonder-filled work of Christ in the entire world and throughout history. This is the stewardship of the grand narrative of God called the Christian faith.

Conclusion

So we conclude as we began: among the goals of each pastor is the desire to foster a community of people marked by specific Christian identity, people whose minds and hearts are joined in the living memory of all that the triune God has done and is doing in Christ through the Spirit. With Christians far and near, we are joined in one faith, one Lord, and one baptism. Church history, deep and wide, provides models for orthodox faith and holy living. As historian Henry Glassie reminds us, history is not just the past but rather a map made up of the past designed to lead us into the future. This is doubly true of church history. As pastors, we are stewards of the map.

Recommended Resources

Dickson, John. *Bullies and Saints: An Honest Look at the Good and Evil in Christian History*. Grand Rapids: Zondervan, 2021.

González, Justo L. *Church History: An Essential Guide*. Nashville: Abingdon Press, 1996.

Ingersol, Stan. *Past and Prospect: The Promise of Nazarene History*. Eugene, OR: Wipf and Stock, 2014.

Pope-Levison, Priscilla. *Models of Evangelism*. Grand Rapids: Baker Academic, 2020.

Shelley, Bruce L. *Church History in Plain Language*. 4th ed. Nashville: Thomas Nelson, 2013.

Snyder, Howard A. "Wesley's Concept of the Church." *Asbury Seminarian* 33, no. 1 (1978): 34-59.

5
STEWARD OF THE CHRISTIAN CREEDS

Stephen G. Green, DMin

WHY SHOULD A PASTOR be a steward of the ancient ecumenical creeds? Answering this question will guide this chapter. The beliefs of a religious community shape its identity and value system. By confessing the creeds, the Christian community is stating its formative faith.

This chapter is meant for the people of God, "for building up the body of Christ, until all of us come to the unity of the faith and of the knowledge of the Son of God, to maturity, to the measure of the full stature of Christ" (Eph. 4:12*b*-13, NRSV). We will discuss the following: *first*, what a creed is; *second*, why creeds are important; *third*, how creeds function as a rule of faith for the church; and *fourth*, ways to employ the creeds in worship and ministry.

We will not trace the historical arguments that led to the Nicene Creed in 325 or any other creed. That history is available in excellent resources.[1] Neither will there be a line-by-line commentary on the creeds.

Together we will discern why a pastor should be a steward of the ancient ecumenical creeds and how he or she can deploy this stewardship.

What Is a Creed?

When people make statements such as "I only believe in the Bible, not some creed," they mistake the meaning of "I believe" as well as the relationship between Canon and creed. Interestingly, the statement "the Bible only" is itself a confession of faith. The English noun "creed" comes from the Latin verb *credo*, which means "I believe." To say "I believe" is a confession of faith. When a confession is formalized, it becomes a creed. Methodist theologian Geoffrey Wainwright explains: "The creeds express the faith that is fundamental to becoming a Christian. They are profoundly doxological, in that they express verbally the substance of the faith of those who, through baptism and beyond, surrender themselves to God in Christ in the life of believing obedience."[2]

The Scriptures and the ecumenical creeds are not mutually exclusive.[3] They are connected for Christians synergistically. A person cannot say "I believe the creeds" without reference to the Scriptures. Conversely, a person or community cannot adequately believe that the God witnessed to in Scripture is triune apart from the creeds hammered out by Christ's church. Credal confession and biblical faith emerged in unison in the early centuries of the Christian faith.

The Christian Bible narrates the story of God as told by Israel and the early church. The ecumenical creeds contain language Christians use to understand who God is as witnessed to in the Bible.[4] This language emerges from the Scriptures and is used to understand the Bible's flesh and blood revelation of God in the person of Jesus the Messiah. For example, the God who created the world, called Israel into existence, freed it from Egyptian bondage, and judged it by exile is revealed in Jesus. Therefore, the creeds functioned as theological grammar for the historic Christian community as it articulated what it believed about God and opposed erroneous beliefs.[5]

The Canon gives its readers the details of the story line of God and creation from beginning to end. The ecumenical creeds tell their confessors how to understand not only who God is but also how Christians fit into the plotline of God's story. Confessors of the Christian creeds live in the time after Jesus's resurrection, as the new creation actively waiting for God's story to be completed.

Three creeds are considered authoritative by the majority of Christian communities. They are universal or ecumenical (from a Greek term meaning "the whole world"). The church universal (Eph. 4:5-6) is united *in* and *by* confessing the creeds. The three creeds are the Apostles' Creed, the Nicene Creed, and the Athanasian Creed. (The Chalcedonian Definition of 451 is also ecumenical[6] but is not written as a creed.) Some branches of Christianity do not confess the Athanasian Creed.[7] So in this chapter when the phrase "ecumenical creeds" is used, it basically refers to the Apostles' Creed and the Nicene Creed. The Nicene Creed confessed in most Christian congregations is actually a reaffirmation by the Council of Constantinople (AD 381) of the creed developed by the Council of Nicaea in AD 325. The Niceno-Constantinopolitan Creed, which explicitly affirms the deity of the Holy Spirit, is the more correct name of the Nicene Creed.

What does it mean to say, "I [or We] believe . . ."? To believe something is to trust what is believed.[8] When a person says "I believe in my spouse," they are voicing their trust. This belief has content—namely, the narrative history of the character of one's spouse. This belief or trust is also confirmed by how the believing spouse lives out this belief in marital life. If, for example, the spouse who claims belief in the other is constantly questioning his or her fidelity, one may rightly wonder if there is genuine trust. For one's beliefs to be reliable, they must be embodied, lived out.

If a community truly believes in the Creator God, then it will embody its faith. God's creation will be treated as a gift from the Creator. If it confesses belief that the one God is definitively revealed in Jesus the Messiah, then its members will live in ways that embody the character of God as disclosed in Jesus. In other words, when the Nicene Creed confesses that the second person of the Godhead is "Jesus Christ, the only son of God, eternally begotten of the Father, God from God, Light from Light, true God from true God,"[9] this is a life-forming affirmation about the character of God.

When reading the New Testament, we observe that in Jesus, God inaugurates his kingdom on earth, touches the unclean, welcomes sinners, eats with outsiders, and challenges the religious elite in Jerusalem. This entails that an embodied witness by a confessing community will also touch the unclean, welcome sinners, eat with outsiders, and challenge the boasts of supremacy of its day. To confess the Christian creeds is to trust the God revealed in Jesus and experienced through the Spirit in an embodied witness called the church.

Why Are Creeds Important?

To answer, we should think of the community of faith beyond one's own ministerial lifespan. What is theologically necessary for ensuring the future vitality of the community of faith?

The ongoing development of the biblical tradition, as expressed in the creeds, implies that one's primary ministerial responsibility is to receive, participate in, and guard apostolic faith and ministry—commonly referred to as the Great Tradition, the truth about Jesus the Messiah proclaimed by the church throughout its history. The apostolic witness is received from the past and extends into the future. Verse 3 of Jude states, "Dear friends, although I was making every effort to write to you concerning our common salvation, I considered it a necessity to write to you to encourage you to contend for the faith delivered once and for all to the saints" (LEB). Faith formation of a historically extended community is dependent upon the ancient confession of who God is and what difference God's identity makes for the people of faith.

Faith formation is enabled exclusively by God's grace—not by an individual or a community. Yet communities and individuals are called to receive this grace by actively participating in the means of grace.

To wait upon the means of grace is to wait among the new-creation people of God, the church. As the church, we participate in Christian practices, stories, and the witness of saints (Heb. 12:1-2). When confessed, the Apostles' Creed and the Nicene Creed encapsulate and practice the Christian story. By confessing its faith, the church retells the story of God and finds its own place in the story. We are not merely reciting a few ancient words.

The words of the creeds are a *speech act* that expresses trust and embodiment of Christian faith. These words about God find their meaning in a socially embodied faith community called the church. The creeds form the identity of this community. They structure the way believers see, feel, and desire. They are a lens through which the church sees the world and itself in the world. The Canon and creeds form the identity of the new-age people of God, the "one holy universal and apostolic church" (Nicene Creed, art. 9).[10] It is the "faith delivered once and for all to the saints" (Jude v. 3, LEB).

How Do the Creeds Function as a Rule of Faith for the Church?

In the earliest days of the postresurrection community, messianic believers read the Old Testament Scriptures as Jesus had taught them. As the New Testament canon emerged, they also read the Gospels and Epistles as Scripture (see ch. 3). From their reading there developed the "rule of faith" (Lat., *regula fidei*), or "the analogy of faith"—a summary of apostolic preaching and teaching. This was the lens—created by the life, death, resurrection, and ascension of Jesus—through which the early church understood the grand story of God as told by Israel and fulfilled in God's Son. The rule of faith was eventually articulated as something that resembles the Apostles' Creed.

The roots of the creeds are observable in the New Testament's use of the Old Testament. Jesus the Messiah was believed to be the beginning of the culminating chapter of the story of God (Acts 2:17). He had been promised throughout the Old Testament (Matt. 26:56; Luke 24:25-27, 44; John 5:39; Rom. 1:16; 1 Cor. 15:3).

As early as the second century, Christians were taught the rule of faith and confessed it as part of their baptism. It formed a foundation for the Apostles' Creed. The rule of faith and the creeds affirm God is One, Father, Son, and Holy Spirit. To enter the new reality, created by Jesus the Messiah, persons confessed this new reality that formed the identity of the community.

The ancient ecumenical creeds are the universal church's rule of faith. They spell out what the church means when it says, "We believe." As Christians confess the creeds, they express their life-forming faith. This is evident in the sacrament of baptism. When a candidate for baptism confesses the Apostles' Creed, she is, by the Spirit, giving herself over to the death and burial of Christ and rising in newness of life with him (Rom. 6:1-11). Questions about who is God, who the baptized are, and how they fit into God's story are answered in baptism. Dying and rising with Christ witnesses to fully trusting the God who creates, redeems, and perfects believers. The baptized become members of the new-age people of God. Early Christianity did not invent its faith but understood the message that Jesus preached and embodied as fulfilling the story of God as told by Israel.

Before looking at the essence of the Apostles' and Nicene Creeds, it will be helpful to review a recurring confession or creed of ancient Israel found in the Old Testament. The creed is first recorded in Exodus 34:6-7 but is found in various forms and whispers in multiple places in the Hebrew Bible (e.g., Num. 14; Deut. 5; 1 Kings 3; Neh. 9; Pss. 103, 145; Jer. 32; Lam. 3; Dan. 9; Jon. 4; Nah. 1). The credal confession describes God's character in relation to human communities and persons. "The LORD, the LORD, the compassionate and gracious God, slow to anger, abounding in love and faithfulness, maintaining love to thousands, and forgiving wickedness, rebellion and sin. Yet he does not leave the guilty unpunished; he punishes the children and their children for the sin of the parents to the third and fourth generation" (Exod. 34:6-7; cf. Deut. 6:4-5, the Shema).

The confession of faith derives from the lived history of Israel, the people of God that began with the originating event in Israel's communal memory, their deliverance from Egyptian bondage. YHWH brought up out of Egypt a band of ragtag slaves and made them God's own people. YHWH gave them Torah, which they defied, and land, which they defiled, and yet God renewed them again and again. This confession or creed has staying power because it rings true in the many episodes in the community's narrative history. YHWH's gracious character is consistent, even toward evil enemies, such as Nineveh. Jonah makes this clear in his closing statements, where he explains why he ran from God: "Isn't this what I said, LORD, when I was still at home? That is what I tried to forestall by fleeing to Tarshish. I knew that you are a gracious and compassionate God, slow to anger and abounding in love, a God who relents from sending calamity" (Jon. 4:2).

Similarly, the premise of the early Christians' confession or rule of faith comes from its lived history with Jesus the Messiah, who announces the inauguration of the kingdom of God and embodies the kingdom in his person. His death, resurrection, and ascension initiate the new age. The Holy Spirit enables believers to participate in God's new creation in a "ministry of reconciliation" (2 Cor. 5:18) as the "born again" (John 3:3). As noted earlier, the rule of faith provided the grammar by which early followers of the postresurrected Jesus "saw" and "participated" in their world.

The life, death, resurrection, and ascension of Jesus are the presuppositions of the New Testament and the creeds, how they understood YHWH. Ancient Israel believed the Creator is the liberating God of the exodus. For the early church the creating, liberating God of Israel is revealed in the person of Jesus the Messiah. He is the Word of God made flesh (John 1:14; 1 John 1:1-4), the express image of God (Col. 1:15). He reveals the God of Israel. "For in him all things were created: things in heaven and on earth, visible and invisible, whether thrones or powers or rulers or authorities; all things have been created through him and for him" (v. 16). No wonder the Nicene Creed confesses "through him all things were made."[11]

The ecumenical creeds affirm that Israel's story of YHWH enters its concluding chapter in Jesus the Messiah. But more than an additional chapter, God's Son and the bestowed Spirit are present and redemptively working out God's will in creation and history "according to [God's] purpose, which he set forth in Christ as a plan for the fullness of time" (Eph. 1:9-10, ESV).

The content of this confession also describes the creation of a new community in the last chapter of God's story, the church. It is no wonder this peculiar people confessed the rule of faith. Through the

Spirit they bore witness to their Lord for all creation, in every place and in all of time. Beginning on the day of Jesus's resurrection, there is a continuation of the apostles' witness (Matt. 28:1-10; Luke 24:1-35). Therefore, the creed confesses that the church is constituted as "one holy universal and apostolic" people.[12]

The faith the church confesses also expresses confident hope for completion of the concluding chapter of YHWH's story. Jesus's resurrection initiated the new age of God's kingdom. But that kingdom has yet to be completed. God's kingdom, like a mustard seed (Matt. 13:31-32) or like yeast in dough (v. 33), is working in the fabric of human history. Creation itself groans for the consummation of this last chapter in God's story when it will be "liberated from its bondage to decay" (Rom. 8:21). The New Testament and the Nicene Creed affirm that Jesus will come to "judge the living and the dead, and his kingdom will have no end."[13] Promise of the kingdom's consummation affirms two things: *first*, how a person lives now matters eternally, and *second*, God in Christ is making the world right.

How to Employ the Creeds in Worship and Ministry

Let's explore two ways to do this: through worship and discernment.

Worship

By leading his or her congregation in reciting the creeds during worship, a pastor cultivates the Christian life and character of a congregation. Character is formed by what and how people worship. For example, if a person or community believes a nation or the family is ultimate, that will become their highest pursued value.

Two related aspects of sin in the Hebrew Scriptures can be explanatory. The *first* is worship of other gods, including treating YHWH as just another god. The *second* is injustice. The categories are connected. If a community worships other gods, it will take on their character (Ps. 135:15-18; Hab. 2:18). If the gods behave abhorrently, the community's way of life will copy their behavior. If the gods control chaos through violence, then the community will do the same. If the gods seek vengeance, so will the worshipping community. If the gods exclude outsiders, then worshippers will shun strangers.

In sharp contrast, the church is called to worship the one true God, who is Father, Son, and Holy Spirit and who graciously loves his creation. In so doing, worshippers become like him.

In the practice of worship, proclaiming the gospel, singing, praying, Scripture reading, and celebrating the sacraments are appointed means of grace, appointed means of formation. In baptism, believers are crucified and buried with Christ and rise in newness of life. The Holy Spirit is poured upon them, and they become a part of the new-age people of God. Through Eucharist, God in Christ becomes uniquely present, enabling the confessing church to participate ever anew in the broken body and shed blood of Jesus. This is both a remembrance of Jesus's reinterpretation of the Passover and an anticipation of his coming again in glory to conclude God's grand story. The "I believe" of the Apostles' Creed, confessed in Baptism, prepares one to confess the "We believe" of the Nicene Creed, confessed by the body during the Eucharist.

In radical contrast to the results of idolatry, in Christian worship, formation in the image of Christ occurs. The creeds are instituted vehicles of worship and formation. Through the Holy Spirit, the confessing church identifies itself with the cross, resurrection, and ascension of Jesus and knows itself as "one holy universal and apostolic" people.[14]

Sadly we must recognize that in its history the church has often failed to live out its identity as "one holy universal and apostolic" people. Its divisions constitute a "scandal" for its witness. But do the divisions disqualify the church as "one holy universal and apostolic"? Are only a few the true church? Is our affirmation of *oneness* only an ascribed fiction? Or is the shared grammar of the creeds, the uniting *rule of faith*, the way we should understand the church's life together—

its identity? Perhaps this is the constitutive form or polity of Christian people, the new community enlivened by the Holy Spirit during this consummating chapter of God's story. This constituting identity is made possible when believers are "baptized" into the death of Christ, released from captivity to the old order and raised to new-creation life in Christ (Rom. 6:1-11). In spite of divisions, Jesus as Lord of all is present in his church, shaping the life of Christians together. Though now enjoyed imperfectly, says Geoffrey Wainwright, the four marks (i.e., "one holy universal and apostolic") anticipate what the church "eschatologically will be."[15]

As God's steward, a pastor is responsible for informing and "re-forming" the people of God in times of worship. The sacraments are pivotal for Christian formation. Confession of the Christian creeds serves the ongoing task of Christian formation and education. This is in harmony with catechizing before baptism, preaching, and teaching in conjunction with the Eucharist and creeds.

Directly or indirectly a pastor can reference the character of God as affirmed in the creeds. Extensive teaching in the context of classes and small groups is important for Christian formation. But so are short moments of instruction in the general course of ministry. Here are two examples of how short phrases can be effective in teaching. *First*, during the celebration of the Eucharist a pastor can remind the congregation: "As the great confession of the church has reminded us, God in his Son, our Savior, is now present with us through bread and cup." *Second*, when preaching from either Testament, reference the revealed character of God. For example, if a pastor is expounding a creation text, remind the congregation that the "Creator has been revealed in the Savior Jesus, our Lord."

Discernment

More than mere knowledge, discernment requires wisdom. Discernment entails opening eyes to see, ears to hear, and lips to speak the word of the Lord. Discernment interprets all reality in light of the new-age kingdom of God declared by and embodied in Jesus the Messiah. Discernment enables the church to see the world aright by first seeing the in-breaking kingdom of God making all things new.[16]

Pastors practice Christian discernment as they preach, counsel, visit, and lead the church in worship and mission. They know and see that the story's protagonist, Jesus Christ, is actively engaging the world today. They lead their congregations in confessing one God, who is Father, Son, and Holy Spirit!

Recommended Resources

Barth, Karl. *Dogmatics in Outline*. New York: Harper and Row, 1959.

Dünzl, Franz. *A Brief History of the Doctrine of the Trinity in the Early Church*. New York: T and T Clark, 2007.

Jenson, Robert W. *Creed and Canon*. Louisville, KY: Westminster John Knox Press, 2010.

Johnson, Luke Timothy. *The Creed: What Christians Believe and Why It Matters*. New York: Doubleday, 2003.

Kelly, J. N. D. *Early Christian Creeds*. London: Longman Group, 1960.

Pelikan, Jaroslav. *Credo: Historical and Theological Guide to Creeds and Confessions of Faith in the Christian Tradition*. New Haven, CT: Yale University Press, 2003.

6
STEWARD OF WORSHIP

Mark R. Quanstrom, PhD

The Church's worship and its vocation to holiness
cannot be separated.[1]

—Geoffrey Wainwright

"HAVE YOU COME to worship?" For almost forty years, that is how I have begun each Sunday worship service I have led. I don't remember when that began or what prompted the question. It may have been motivated by the simple need to transition from announcements to the worship service proper. Regardless of the original intention, I have come to appreciate the importance of the question. I will continue to ask it for this reason: worship is the central Christian response to the salvation of our Lord. By asking the question at the beginning of the worship service, God's people are reminded of the singular importance of worship and the principal reason the Lord has brought us together.

Granted, worship of God includes more than Sunday worship. The apostle Paul informed the Christians in Rome that their entire lives should be an act of worship. "Therefore, I urge you, brothers and sisters, in view of God's mercy, to offer your bodies as a living sacrifice, holy and pleasing to God—this is your true and proper worship" (Rom. 12:1). There is to be no segmentation of worship between church and daily life; every aspect of our lives should express gratitude and praise to God, who is redeeming us. Geoffrey Wainwright observes that "in worship we take in the outpouring of God's creative and redemptive love, and we offer in return our thanks and supplications."[2] Into worship, "people bring their entire existence so that it may be gathered up in praise."[3] It is the preeminent time for pondering and learning to apply the Scriptures.[4] From worship, Christians "depart with a renewed vision of the value-patterns of God's kingdom [intending] to glorify God in their whole life."[5] In worship, the church meets with Christ and "[learns] *from him* what sort of Bride it is that he loves."[6] For this reason, from the beginning Christians have gathered in community to worship the God of their salvation.

Today, some people dismiss the importance of God's people gathering for worship. To my mind that amounts to dismissing specific periods of prayer because we are instructed to "pray without ceasing" (1 Thess. 5:17, KJV). One does not exclude the other. Just as there is a

75

greater likelihood of ceaseless prayer when there are designated times for prayer, so there is a greater likelihood of all life becoming an act of worship if there are designated times for focused corporate worship.

The Lord's Day

The New Testament is clear. Worship is central to the Christian life. After Jesus's resurrection, his disciples gathered for worship. Matthew records, "Then the eleven disciples went to Galilee, to the mountain where Jesus had told them to go. When they saw him, they worshiped him" (Matt. 28:16-17). Subsequent to Jesus's ascension, Luke records, "Then [the disciples] worshiped him and returned to Jerusalem with great joy. And they stayed continually at the temple, praising God" (Luke 24:52-53). Worship as praise and gratitude was the initial and inevitable response to the resurrected and ascended Lord.

The early church believed the most appropriate day to worship the risen Lord was Sunday because on that day, by the power of the Holy Spirit, the Father raised Jesus from the dead. Since Jesus was "Lord of the Sabbath" (Matt. 12:8), worshipping on Sunday reinforced that lordship. Early Christians thought of the Lord's Day as the first day of the new creation (John 1:1; 20:1) and the eighth day of creation, or the day of new beginnings. Sunday was Easter every week! By worshipping on Sunday, Christians explicitly bore witness to the supremacy of Christ. He, not Caesar and not empire, is Lord (Gk., *Kyrios*) of all. There was nothing subtle about their affirmation.

Although Paul discouraged a legalistic interpretation of special days (Rom. 14:5), he did recognize the first day of the week as the Lord's Day. According to Acts 20:7-12, while visiting Christians in Troas, Paul preached "on the first day of the week" (v. 7) and preached so long that a young man named Eutychus fell asleep, tumbled out of a third-floor window, died, and was resuscitated by Paul. When he instructed the Corinthian Christians to "set aside a sum of money in keeping with your income," he told them to do that when they gathered for worship "on the first day of every week" (1 Cor.

16:2). The most notable mention of the first day of the week for worship occurs in Revelation 1:10: John was "in the Spirit on the Lord's day" (KJV). The church has celebrated Christ's resurrection as the new Sabbath ever since.

Because neither Romans nor Jews recognized Sunday as a special day, Christians gathered early in the morning before going off to work—often before sunrise. The Lord's Day was not meant to mimic the Jewish Sabbath as a "day of rest." Instead, by worshipping on Sunday, Christians were bearing witness to Jesus's resurrection.

What Did Early Christians Do as They Worshipped?

The New Testament and other first-century documents tell us those early Christians did six things as they worshipped.

First, they sang. Geoffrey Wainwright says their hymns were "sung confession[s]."[7] They sang psalms, as some of them had done in the synagogue. After the Lord's Supper, Jesus and his disciples sang a hymn before going to the Mount of Olives to pray (Matt. 26:30; Mark 14:26). According to the apostle Paul, singing evidenced the life of the Spirit in believers. He instructed the Christians in Ephesus to be "filled with the Spirit, speaking to one another with psalms, hymns, and songs from the Spirit. Sing and make music from your heart to the Lord" (Eph. 5:18-19). Paul even gave directions for the song service. In an instruction about how to conduct an orderly worship service, he told the believers at Corinth to come prepared: "When you come together, each of you has a hymn, or a word of instruction, a revelation" (1 Cor. 14:26). Many scholars believe that in his instruction to the Christians at Philippi about their love for each other, Paul quoted a hymn (Phil. 2:6-11). Colossians 1:15-20; 1 Timothy 3:16; Hebrews 1:1-3; and 1 Peter 2:21-25 might also be early hymns of the church. Clearly, singing praises to their risen Lord formed an essential part of their worship.

Second, Christians collected offerings. Paul's instruction to the church at Corinth about the collection for the poor Christians in Jerusalem has been mentioned. Earlier in that letter Paul encouraged the Corinthians to give generously. "Each of you should give what you have decided in your heart to give, not reluctantly or under compulsion, for God loves a cheerful giver" (2 Cor. 9:7). Because of Christian generosity, Luke could report, "There were no needy persons among them. For from time to time those who owned land or houses sold them, brought the money from the sales and put it at the apostles' feet, and it was distributed to anyone who had need" (Acts 4:34-35). Christians gave generously as tangible evidence of gratitude for what they had received from their Lord and as evidence of love for others.

Third, Christians prayed. Prayer was one of the first reasons Christians gathered. Luke reports that after Jesus's ascension the disciples joyously returned to Jerusalem "and were continually in the temple blessing God" (Luke 24:53, RSV). Luke also records a prayer the young church offered after the priests, captain of the temple, and the Sadducees released Peter and John. The prayer begins, "Sovereign Lord, who didst make the heaven and the earth and the sea and everything in them . . ." (Acts 4:24-30, RSV).

To the Corinthians, Paul gave specific instructions about prayer (1 Cor. 11:2-16). They prayed the Lord's Prayer, and they prayed the Psalms. They prayed before and after the sacrament of the Lord's Supper. They sometimes prayed extemporaneously. Christians interceded for each other, and they were instructed to pray for all those in authority (1 Tim. 2:2). Clearly, prayer formed an essential part of Christian worship.

Fourth, Christians read the Scriptures in their worship services. In the beginning, they read aloud the only Scriptures they had at the time, the Septuagint, the Greek translation of the Old Testament. Then, as Paul and other apostles began writing letters to individual churches, they, too, were read aloud when Christians gathered and then copied and circulated among other churches. Paul instructed the Christians in Thessalonica: "I charge you before the Lord to have this letter read to all the brothers and sisters" (1 Thess. 5:27). He told the church in Colossae, "After this letter has been read to you, see that it is also read in the church of the Laodiceans and that you in turn read the letter from Laodicea" (Col. 4:16).

Soon the early church began to read Paul's letters as Scripture. In an intriguing passage, the apostle Peter wrote, "Bear in mind that our Lord's patience means salvation, just as our dear brother Paul also wrote you with the wisdom that God gave him. He writes the same way in all his letters, speaking in them of these matters. His letters contain some things that are hard to understand, which ignorant and unstable people distort, as they do the other Scriptures, to their own destruction" (2 Pet. 3:15-16).

Most of the books that compose the New Testament were meant for congregations, not for individuals. Epaphroditus carried Paul's cordial letter to the church in Philippi, where it was read to the congregation. Phoebe, a deacon from Cenchreae (near Corinth), carried Paul's letter to the house churches in Rome. She would have read and explained it to them (Rom. 16:1-2). Congregations studied the documents, and the documents informed Christians about their newfound faith and, through the Spirit, built them up in the "most holy faith" (Jude v. 20).

Since the Bible would not become readily available until the printing press in the fifteenth century, the public reading of Scripture was the only way that Christians could have heard it. The Scriptures were so precious to them that during the Roman persecutions, Christians chose to die rather than surrender their treasured Scriptures to the authorities. Christians have listened to the Word of God read in their worship services on the Lord's Day for two thousand years.

Fifth, Christians heard expositions of the Scriptures through a sermon. Preaching was a priority. It is sometimes forgotten that Jesus referred to himself as a preacher. To the disciples who wanted Jesus to "stay put," he responded, "'Let us go somewhere else—to the nearby villages—so I can preach there also. That is why I have come.'

So he traveled throughout Galilee, preaching in their synagogues and driving out demons" (Mark 1:38-39).

The apostle Paul also understood himself to be first of all a preacher, a proclaimer of the good news of Jesus Christ. He told the Corinthians, "Woe to me if I do not preach the gospel!" (1 Cor. 9:16b).

The apostle Peter's first activity after the disciples received the promised Holy Spirit on the day of Pentecost was to proclaim the gospel, using Joel 2:28-32 as his text (Acts 2:14-40). After Cornelius explained why he had sent for Peter (10:30-33), Peter began to preach: "I now realize how true it is that God does not show favoritism" (v. 34; see also vv. 35-43). He explained that Jesus had commanded the apostles "to preach to the people and to testify that he is the one whom God appointed as judge of the living and the dead" (v. 42; cf. Mark 3:14). Following the example of the Lord and the apostles, the first-century church understood the importance of the preached word.

Sixth, they received the Lord's Supper, the Eucharist. Evidence indicates this happened each time Christians gathered for worship. Paul gave clear instructions to the church in Corinth:

> For I received from the Lord what I also passed on to you: The Lord Jesus, on the night he was betrayed, took bread, and when he had given thanks, he broke it and said, "This is my body, which is for you; do this in remembrance of me." In the same way, after supper he took the cup, saying, "This cup is the new covenant in my blood; do this, whenever you drink it, in remembrance of me." For whenever you eat this bread and drink this cup, you proclaim the Lord's death until he comes. (1 Cor. 11:23-26)

Although Paul was not present during the first Lord's Supper, he insisted he had received instruction from the Lord himself.

According to Paul, the Eucharist not only was a dramatic way to remember Jesus's death but also, in the Spirit's power, reenacts our Lord's death. In a way, we cannot fully explain how the risen and ascended Christ is redemptively present in the Lord's Supper, which is why Paul insisted that it be observed in holy reverence and in order (vv. 27-34). He believed that Christ was present in the Eucharist event, just as he had been present on the night of his betrayal.

These six practices—singing, giving an offering, praying, listening to Scripture, proclamation, and celebrating the Eucharist—constituted early Christian worship. Luke summarized the practices of the early church in Acts 2, when he wrote, "They devoted themselves to the apostles' teaching and to fellowship, to the breaking of bread and to prayer. . . . All the believers were together and had everything in common. They sold property and possessions to give to anyone who had need" (vv. 42, 44-45).

Their devotion to the "apostles' teaching" was indicative of their commitment to listening to the spoken words of the apostles living at the time, which then included listening to their writings being read.

Their devotion to "fellowship" evidenced their commitment to the community of faith, to the *koinonia*. Though individuals certainly had a personal relationship with the resurrected Lord, Christian faith was communal, not individualistic. There were no "solitary" Christians, no private, self-defined relationships with Jesus Christ. There was one body with many members. Christians were so committed to each other in the community that they even sold property and possessions to tend to the needs of their sisters and brothers.

Their devotion to the "breaking of bread" evidenced their commitment to the sacrament of the Lord's Supper. Celebrated in the gathering of God's people for worship, the Eucharist affirmed the necessity of community for Christian faith. As it was with the sacrament of baptism, so it was with the sacrament of the Lord's Supper: the Eucharist cannot be administered by oneself.

And their "devotion to prayer" evidenced confident communion with the triune God. Devotion "to the apostles' teaching and to fellowship, to the breaking of bread and to prayer" (v. 42) characterized worship in the New Testament church.

Consequences of Christian Worship

There were at least four major consequences of worship in the New Testament.

First, and most importantly, through the Holy Spirit, the risen Lord was present. Christ was really present, contemporaneous with them as Redeemer, as "Lord of all" (Acts 10:36). They gathered to worship because they wanted to be with their risen Lord. They knew Jesus would be present, for he had gathered his people.

This is what Jesus said would happen. Before his crucifixion, Jesus told his disciples that he was leaving but that he would return to them through the ministry of the Holy Spirit. "I will not leave you as orphans; I will come to you. Before long, the world will not see me anymore, but you will see me. Because I live, you also will live. On that day you will realize that I am in my Father, and you are in me, and I am in you" (John 14:18-20). According to Matthew, the Christ who was "God with us" at the beginning of Matthew's Gospel (1:23) promised to be "God with us" always, to the end of the age (28:20). Christ was with worshippers on the Lord's Day, in the reading of the written Word, in the preached word, in the sacrament, in each other! They knew that if they wanted to be with Jesus, they would be where he had gathered his people.

The *second* consequence of worship was that through the Spirit, Christians were formed in the image of Christ. They were being made holy, sanctified in Christ (1 Cor. 1:2). Believers learned how to be grateful, how to pray, and how to love and mentor each other. In short, they were being thoroughly *evangelized,* which meant discipled by the Holy Spirit.

The *third* consequence of the church gathering for worship was that they became a sign of the inaugurated and coming kingdom of God. In Jesus of Nazareth, God transformatively entered human history, into a fallen creation, and inaugurated his promised kingdom on earth. As the people of God gathered, they were the visible evidence that new creation had begun. They were a countercultural community, witnessing to the King of kings and Lord of all.

Thus Christian worship bore no semblance to a gathering in an amphitheater. It was not an aggregation of individuals. Rather, it was a disciplined community of faith, made one in common confession, created in Christ Jesus to be his living body in the world, the evidence of his resurrection, embodying the character of Jesus.

The *fourth* consequence of worship was the fulfilling of the mission. Worship was missional! In response to devotion to the apostles' teaching, to fellowship in the Spirit, to breaking the bread, and to prayer, Christians bore witness in the world. And "the Lord added to their number daily those who were being saved" (Acts 2:47). As history bears witness, they "[made] disciples of all the nations, baptizing them in the name of the Father and of the Son and of the Holy Spirit, teaching them to observe all things" Jesus commanded; and Jesus was with them (Matt. 28:16-29, NKJV).

The Responsibility of the Pastor in Christian Worship

One of the unanticipated consequences of asking my congregation every week the same question, "Have you come to worship?" was that I began taking more seriously my responsibility for providing a worship service that was worthy of the resurrected Lord. Preparation for that worship service took priority. If worship is the central Christian response to the salvation of our Lord, and if worship is where the resurrected Lord is present, where God's people are formed in his image as a sign of the kingdom, then clearly the worship service deserved more careful consideration and preparation than I had been providing.

One afternoon I was reflecting on my responsibility as worship leader. I had an unmistakable encounter with the Lord that changed how I understood my responsibility for worship services. As I was praying for direction, the Lord said, "You need to be more afraid of me than of your people." As I processed that encounter, I realized my deliberations about how to lead the church had primarily been driven by pragmatic interests. I was more focused on what I thought would be acceptable to my congregation than on what the Lord wanted. Specifically, in my preparation for preaching, I had been more invested in what I believed would please the congregation than I was in what would please the Lord. I realized I had been thus editing the gospel. In my convicting encounter with the Lord, I learned I was to preach the whole counsel of God and not simply what I preferred or what I thought would be acceptable to the people.

Frankly, I did not know how to do that. Putting before my people the whole counsel of God was formidable. But by desiring to be obedient, I discovered the *Revised Common Lectionary*. A lectionary is simply a schedule of Scripture readings to be read during the weekly worship service. Lectionary readings have been used by the church from the beginning, based upon their use in the synagogue. In the New Testament there is evidence of its use. The Isaiah text Jesus read in the synagogue as the basis for his first sermon (Luke 4:16-27) was likely the prescribed reading for that day.

The Christian lectionary is a three-year schedule of four Scripture passages to be read each Sunday. There is an Old Testament passage, a psalm, an epistle reading, and a gospel reading. The lectionary readings are thematically related and indexed to the seasons of the church year. The lectionary narrates the story of God and provides for God's people a comprehensive hearing of the story. In light of the church's ancient tradition of reading Scripture in worship services, and in response to God's instruction to me, it was a relatively simple decision to begin incorporating lectionary readings into our worship services. It had not occurred to me before that generally greater attention is given to Scripture in liturgical traditions than it is in many "Bible-believing" churches.

The benefits of regular lectionary readings in worship services are numerous.

First, it highlights the priority of the written Word. If the Bible is not important enough to be read on the Lord's Day, then perhaps it isn't important enough to be read during the week. Our Western culture is increasingly biblically illiterate. If people are not hearing the Bible read on Sunday, they are probably not reading it or hearing it any other day.

Second, my experience as pastor is that hearing the written Word can be the most formative part of worship services. There is transformative power in hearing Scripture read without commentary.

I learned that just as God began creation with a divine word, even so by the Spirit he still creates through the words of Scripture. People are comforted and convicted as Scripture is read. As promised, it does not return empty (Isa. 55:11).

Third, using the lectionary compels a pastor to submit to the Scriptures instead of becoming "lord of the Scriptures." By following the lectionary, the preacher no longer decides what people need to hear from God's Word. Obviously he or she must discern what God wants people to hear; the lectionary is God's servant. The lectionary—to borrow what Jesus said about the Sabbath—was made for people, not people for the lectionary. Still, the discipline of preaching from prescribed texts protects against the temptation to manipulate God's Word—that is, to further a preacher's own agenda. I fear the commandment preachers most often abuse is the third one against the taking of the Lord's name in vain. Moses was told, "The LORD will not hold anyone guiltless who misuses his name" (Exod. 20:7*b*). No matter how well intended, using God's Word to accomplish a personal agenda violates the third commandment. Preaching from texts one has not personally chosen helps protect against misappropriating the Word of God.

Fourth, and perhaps most importantly, using the lectionary reminds the church that the Christian faith is not ours to do with as we wish. It is to be carefully stewarded. The apostle Paul wrote, "For what I received I passed on to you" (1 Cor. 15:3*a*). The text reminds us that the church is the steward of the Christian faith. It has received

85

the gospel message from others who were faithful. We must faithfully transmit it to others.

Reading carefully chosen texts in the assembly on the Lord's Day reminds us that our faith is an ancient and communal faith for which we pastors are stewards.

Fifth, reading prescribed lectionary texts not only provides continuity with those who have preceded us but also places us in fellowship with believers worldwide who are reading the same texts. The lectionary reminds us that the church is *catholic*, universally one Lord, one faith, and one baptism, and that through the Spirit we are in communion with all our sisters and brothers worldwide.

My discovery also helped me realize that I must incorporate confession of the ecumenical creeds, praying the Lord's Prayer, regularly celebrating the Lord's Supper, and employing the classic hymns, as well as choruses, that teach the faith. Theological faithfulness to the whole counsel of God took precedence over other considerations.

The result of these commitments was contrary to what I anticipated. I witnessed among my people an increasing desire for worship. A deeper sense of God's presence developed. Worship became more a "means" of God's sanctifying grace. Awareness of *koinonia*, being the body of Christ, increased. My congregants valued sermons based on the lectionary, knowing their pastor was submitting to the Scriptures as well. In response to hearing the Bible systematically read on Sundays, my people began to read the Bible more faithfully. By confessing the creeds, my people learned what is of first importance. The Lord's Supper became more meaningful. And I became a better steward of the faith.

After leading worship in ways that more faithfully reflected the tradition of the church catholic, one of my leaders summarized the congregation's response. She simply said, "Finally!"

Conclusion

Worship of the triune God is *the* believer's response to redemption. The question "Have you come to worship?" is not only appropriate for the Lord's Day but also the most important question of our lives. In all ways, Paul says, "We have come to worship" (see Rom. 12:1-3).

Pastors, we are irreplaceable stewards of the worship of our resurrected Lord.

Recommended Resources

Bevins, Winfield. *Ever Ancient, Ever New*. Grand Rapids: Zondervan, 2019.

Christian Resource Institute. The Voice: Biblical and Theological Resources for Growing Christians. Accessed March 12, 2022. http://www.crivoice.org/index.html.

Kreider, Alan. *The Patient Ferment of the Early Church*. Grand Rapids: Baker Academic, 2016.

Miller, Barbara Day. *Encounters with the Holy: A Conversational Model for Worship Planning*. Herndon, VA: Alban Institute, 2010.

Neuhaus, Richard John. *Freedom for Ministry*. Grand Rapids: Eerdmans, 1992.

Peterson, Brent D. *Created to Worship: God's Invitation to Become Fully Human*. Kansas City: Beacon Hill Press of Kansas City, 2012.

Stevens, John G., and Michael Waschevski. *Rhythms of Worship: The Planning and Purpose of Liturgy*. Louisville, KY: Westminster John Knox Press, 2014.

Vanderbilt Divinity Library. *Revised Common Lectionary*. Accessed March 12, 2022. https://lectionary.library.vanderbilt.edu/index.php.

Wainwright, Geoffrey. *Doxology: The Praise of God in Worship, Doctrine, and Life*. New York: Oxford University Press, 1980.

Online Lectionary Resources

Calvin Theological Seminary. Center for Excellence in Preaching. Accessed March 12, 2022. https://cep.calvinseminary.edu/.

The Lectionary Page. Accessed March 12, 2022. https://www.lectionarypage.net/index.html.

Luther Seminary. Working Preacher. Accessed March 12, 2022. https://www.workingpreacher.org/.

A Plain Account. Your Wesleyan Lectionary Resource. Accessed March 12, 2022. http://www.aplainaccount.org/

7

STEWARD OF THE SACRAMENTS

Diane Leclerc, PhD

THE THEME of this book is that pastors are vital agents in teaching and preaching the Christian faith, including their theological tradition. The faith is passed down and placed in pastors' hands to hold and cherish. However, fidelity to the faith and to one's theological tradition misses the mark unless both are carefully applied to the contexts in which we conduct our sacred work. We must hold our theology deeply within our hearts and minds and wisely apply its principles to parishioners' lives. We must "rub the faith into" all the nooks and crannies of human experience. Unless theology is purposefully deployed by pastors, it will die.

As a theological steward, being a good steward of the Christian sacraments is imperative but can at times seem daunting. How does one harness a mystery?

The Sacraments in the Wesleyan-Holiness Tradition

When treating the sacraments in the Wesleyan-holiness tradition, we are faced with numerous questions. Among the first is whether or not we are a sacramental tradition. Rob Staples notes that Wesleyan-holiness denominations come from two different traditions that do not always agree.[1] On the one hand, the Wesleys were part of the Anglican Church, just one step away from the weighty sacramentalism of Roman Catholicism. On the other hand, John Wesley was deeply influenced by Pietism. Moravian Pietism helped him understand the heartfelt inner assurance of salvation (e.g., his 1738 Aldersgate experience). Pietism was much less sacramental and eventually nonsacramental for some branches. Pietists did not view the sacraments as central to and definitive of Christian faith. Instead, the sacraments were considered secondary to personal conversion and discipleship embodied in spiritual disciplines. Wesley and the Moravians eventually separated. The Moravians' "weak" view of the Lord's Supper was a factor.

Wesley strongly believed the sacraments are essential for Christian life. But as Methodism expanded in the American colonies, the primary emphasis was on evangelism. The practice of baptism and Communion was more urgent than articulating a sacramental theology.

What has changed since the nineteenth-century holiness movement? Do we lean into our Anglican heritage or into our pietistic and revivalist roots? Staples sees a tension between "structure" and "spirit" that results in a "dilemma."[2] The holiness movement, he observes, "never worked out for itself any thoroughgoing theology of the sacraments."[3] For many in our tradition the sacraments appear optional, even the sacrament of baptism.

So our question is, How sacramental should we be? Ironically, what Jesus instituted as a unifying practice for his followers has become divisive. There is significant disagreement about the sacraments in Christianity, including our Wesleyan-holiness tradition. This raises numerous questions.[4]

What Is a Sacrament?

Countless books have been written about the nature of the sacraments, from many historical and theological perspectives. Here history and theology go together. Major historical shifts, such as occurred during the Protestant Reformation, introduced multiple changes in sacramental theology.

Is it still possible to articulate the essence, the *mystery* of the sacraments? Admittedly, no one fully understands what happens in and through the sacraments, but throughout nearly two thousand years of Christian history, Christians have affirmed that God uses the sacraments in a unique way to strengthen participants and the church universal. Throughout its history, the church (excepting those who reject the sacraments) has instituted *sacred* (*sacra*-mental) practices or rituals as distinctive conduits of God's presence and grace.

A sacrament can be defined as an instituted practice in which God is potently and uniquely present and active. Although the Catholic Church affirms more sacraments, most of Protestant Christianity affirms baptism and Eucharist as special means of grace—outward signs of an inward invisible grace. Robert Jenson defines the sacraments as "visible words" of gospel and grace as distinct from "spoken words" of gospel and grace.[5]

A Brief Historical Overview

A short historical review is helpful. The church was largely one until its first split in 1054 CE between the Roman Catholic Church in the West and the Orthodox Church in the East. Before then, a shared theology of the sacraments had developed. In the Catholic Church in the thirteenth century, Thomas Aquinas borrowed from Aristotelian philosophy for his *clarification* of how the church should explain the Eucharist. Its position is known as transubstantiation, an explanation of what happens in the bread and cup when a priest consecrates them. In sum, transubstantiation is the belief that the *essence* of the Eucharistic elements literally changes into Christ's body and blood, but the visible *accidents* (taste, texture, appearance) of the elements remain unchanged. The Catholic Church also affirms the sacrament of baptism. After catechism, Catholics will baptize anyone ready to join their faith community. Infant baptism is most frequently practiced. Its theological rationale traces to Augustine (354–430) in his development of the doctrine of original sin.

The Protestant Reformation encompassed more than one "Reformation." The *Lutheran* Reformation rejected and changed many Catholic beliefs and practices. Consubstantiation is the official Lutheran understanding of the Eucharist. This means Christ is present in, with, and under the bread and wine when the Eucharist is celebrated. An analogy has been used that is helpful here, as articulated in a book by Gregg Allison. To explain consubstantiation he points to a sponge and water. "Wherever a sponge is that's soaked with water, there is the water. And wherever the water is, it's there contained by the sponge. The sponge is not the water, the water is not the sponge but the two are there together."[6] Luther said the "Word of God" for the "forgiveness of sins" is "the chief thing in the sacrament." "If the sacrament is rightly administered, one should preach that the sacrament *is* the body and blood *under* the bread and wine."[7] The Lutherans also continued to baptize infants.

In the *Calvinist* wing of the Reformation "substantiation" theology ended. John Calvin (1509-64) believed that when we receive Communion, Christ is really present in the elements. But they do not change. This is usually referred to as "real presence." It would be appropriate to say that the bread and wine are symbols. Symbols do not just point to something, but they participate in that to which they point. Although Zwingli (see below) also believed in a type of symbolism, his use of symbol points to the event of Christ's passion, which we remember. For Calvin, the symbols are active as we take them. They deliver to us a truly present Christ. How is this possible? Calvin believed it is a mystery. But he theorizes that when we serve Communion, the church is mysteriously lifted, through the Holy Spirit, into the presence of Christ, who is at God's right hand in heaven. A second idea is that the Holy Spirit enables Christ to descend "into" the elements when the church celebrates the Lord's Supper, and makes Christ present. The Calvinist, or Reformed, Reformation continued infant baptism, but its meaning began to shift.

The *Swiss* Reformation is sometimes squeezed between the Calvinist Reformation and the Anabaptist Reformation, but it was in fact distinct. We associate the Swiss Reformation with the theology of Ulrich Zwingli (1484-1531). He is credited with developing a Eucharistic theology called the "memorialist" position. Zwingli not only argued against the Catholic doctrine of transubstantiation but also opposed the positions of Luther and Calvin. He believed the bread and wine of the Eucharist are "signifiers" of what Christ has done for us. They *remind* us (thus the word "memorial") of Christ's sacrifice on our behalf. The conduit of grace is in our remembering, not in the elements themselves. This distinction kept Luther and Zwingli from joining forces in the Protestant movement. Zwingli practiced infant

baptism, a fact that separated him from the next form of Protestant-
ism, the *Radical* Reformation, also known as the *Anabaptist* tradition.

The word "anabaptist" means "rebaptizer." The Anabaptists
strictly opposed infant baptism. They cast off the belief that infant
baptism conveys a "grace-full" benefit to infants. They believed that
infant baptism beguiled people into thinking they are Christians just
because they have been baptized. Anabaptists urged upon everyone
who would follow Christ a *believer's* baptism, even if they had been
baptized as infants. Interestingly, the official denominations that
emerged from the Anabaptists are not the ones that reject infant
baptism in today's popular evangelicalism. Members of one Anabaptist denomination—the Quakers—reject both sacraments. The popu-
larity of the memorialist view of Communion and an Anabaptist view
of baptism prominent in today's evangelicalism would be puzzling
were we not to shift our attention from continental Europe to the
English Reformation—to the rise of Anglicanism and its offshoots.

In brief, in British Christianity numerous theological conflicts
erupted before it achieved the Anglican "middle way" under Queen
Elizabeth I (1533–1603). Some of these conflicts drove people to seek
practice of their beliefs elsewhere. The Puritans, who did not seek
separation from the Church of England, and the separatist Pilgrims
(radical Puritans) settled much of New England. From Puritan theology arises parts of the Baptist movement. Some Baptist denominations joined a theology of rebaptism with the theology of Calvin;
others, with the theology of Jacobus Arminius, such as the Freewill
Baptists. The more recent nondenominational movement reflects
much of Baptist theology, especially believer-only baptism.

Where does John Wesley fit into these diverse sacramental the-
ologies? Clearly, Wesley derives most of his sacramental theology
from the Anglican Church, which affirmed the sacraments as "an
outward and visible sign of an inward and spiritual grace given to us,
ordained by Christ himself, as a means whereby we receive the same,
and a pledge to assure us thereof."[8] Like Calvin, Anglicans affirmed

the "real presence."[9] They affirmed the Eucharist as a *means of grace,* especially *sanctifying* grace. John Wesley believed this strongly.

Did John Wesley change the Anglican position in any way? Yes and no. If we simply read the Anglican liturgy, we won't find much difference. Wesley continued to use this liturgy. But it could be argued that he also placed greater emphasis on the presence of the Holy Spirit in Eucharistic worship than did the Anglican Church. Calvin certainly references the Holy Spirit in his understanding of real presence. But there seems to be an urgency or passion about the Spirit's activity as seen in the Wesleys' epiclesis hymns and prayers, just as there is in Wesley's Methodist revival overall. A second shift is practical rather than theological. It is found in Wesley's willingness to break with the Anglican Church in the American Colonies when Anglican priests abandoned its members during the Revolutionary War. Wesley ordained priests as Methodists to provide the Eucharist for Methodists. And he affirmed infant baptism as the primary way English people were baptized.

The Sacraments in the Church of the Nazarene

The preceding brief history brings us *to* and *through* the American holiness movement to today. Before continuing, however, we should remember our theology must be correlated with real life experiences. Where sacramental theology is perhaps most uncertain among us is in *practicing* our theology in the church. Thus the questions below have theological and practical importance.[10]

Eucharist (Holy Communion, the Lord's Supper)[11]

For many decades the article of faith of the Church of the Nazarene on the Lord's Supper (art. XIII) used the word "memorial" in its definition. In 2017 the language changed: "The Lord's Supper is a means of grace in which Christ is present by the Spirit."[12] The ritual also changed and now uses the new language. The change is more consistent with Wesley's position; it moves away from Zwingli's position.

This raises three questions.

First, how is this sacrament *efficacious* for us? What is God "up to" as we receive Holy Communion? Most importantly, we believe the Eucharist is an active *means of grace,* not just a sign or symbol that reminds us that grace comes through Christ's sacrifice. Rather, God is active in and through the sacrament, not just in our minds as we remember Christ's sacrifice. The bread and cup are means, or conduits of whatsoever grace we need. Also, we Nazarenes have maintained the position of real presence by adding the phrase "present by the Spirit" to remind us that the Spirit is indeed active in the sacrament, which corresponds with the strong pneumatology in our tradition. The sacrament is *efficacious* because of the work of Christ made present through the Spirit in receiving the sacrament.

Second, who has *access* to Holy Communion? Here language in the 2017-21 edition of the *Manual* also changed. The previous wording was, "It is distinctly for those who are prepared for reverent appreciation of its significance." Most pastors interpreted this to mean the Eucharist is for Christians only. The new wording is, "All are invited to participate by faith in Christ and be renewed." The reason for the change relies upon one aspect of Wesley's theology of the Eucharist. He implied the Lord's Supper can become a "converting ordinance," which means the Eucharist can be a person's *first* step of faith toward conversion.

In some respects, this is a radical position. For example, who is permitted to receive Communion in say a Lutheran or Anglican church? Only those who are believers, as witnessed by their baptism. We Nazarenes are already "radical" in not first requiring baptism, but even more so in viewing the Eucharist's potential for conversion. We believe no matter where a person is on the Christian journey, grace is available through faith, and the Lord's Supper can be an occasion for receiving transforming grace.

Two additional points regarding accessibility are important. How old should a person be? And what does it mean to receive Communion "unworthily"?

An argument is often made that children should not receive Communion because they do not understand. This might be a legitimate argument. It is up to a pastor to decide how she or he will handle this topic, for it is not addressed in our Articles of Faith. On the other hand, do any of us really understand the mystery of the sacraments? Perhaps absence of full understanding should not be a barrier.

Also, it is erroneous theology to insist that a person must be spiritually "fit" to receive Communion. This has had the unfortunate result of frightening people away from the Lord's Table. Sound exegesis reveals that "spiritually fit" is not what Paul is referring to in 1 Corinthians 11:27-32. If the Eucharist is a means of grace, then the perfect place to be—even run toward—is the Communion Table. Analogously, insisting on being "spiritually fit" would amount to saying we need to bathe before we take a bath! We cannot make ourselves right with God; that is a work of grace. And at least for Wesley Eucharist was the most important means of grace. It is most appropriate that repentance and confession occur while receiving the elements.

Third, how often should we receive the Lord's Supper? And, related to that, how often should it be offered or celebrated? *First*, a bit of history is helpful. When Methodism began increasing, there were not enough ordained ministers to offer the Lord's Supper frequently. There were scores of lay preachers but very few ordained Methodist ministers. Often ministers would have a circuit, which meant they were responsible for multiple congregations. They rode by horseback to a different congregation each week. Instructions were given that ministers should visit churches and serve Communion at least once a quarter. Not surprisingly, "once a quarter" became the norm. But the norm did not change once congregations had their own ministers. Consequently, some holiness denominations continue to offer Communion only four times a year. *Second*, a reason given for not receiving the Eucharist more frequently is that it will lose its significance. Wesley faced this argument and wrote a sermon in response: "The Duty of Constant Communion." Because the Eucharist is a means of grace like other means of grace, opposing frequent reception is like saying, "We should not read our Bibles or pray very often, for doing so might lose its significance." There is no mandate for frequency, but a pastor should consider the following: He or she is steward of the Eucharist—the only one who can administer it, according to two thousand years of practice. Is there not a sense of (eternal) accountability if a minister minimizes opportunities for this means of grace?

One place where pastors can live into this accountability for what has been entrusted to them is in the *administration* of the sacraments, especially Eucharist. Foremost, it must be administered with a proper sense of sanctity. This does not mean this aspect of the service must be overly somber or shaming. It is too easy for a pastor to so concentrate on our guilt that forgiveness as the primary message of this visible sign is overpowered. In fact shaming has kept many persons from coming to the Communion Table. It is most appropriate to offer assurance of forgiveness in the liturgy. We can learn from the Book of Common Prayer.

Hear the Word of God to all who truly turn to him.

Come unto me, all ye that travail and are heavy laden, and I will refresh you. *Matthew 11:28*

God so loved the world, that he gave his only-begotten Son, to the end that all that believe in him should not perish, but have everlasting life. *John 3:16*

This is a true saying, and worthy of all men to be received, that Christ Jesus came into the world to save sinners. *1 Timothy 1:15*

If any man sin, we have an Advocate with the Father, Jesus Christ the righteous; and he is the perfect offering for our sins, and not for ours only, but for the sins of the whole world. *1 John 2:1-2*[13]

Baptism

First, let's consider infant baptism. In denominations of the holiness movement there is diversity in baptism, especially infant baptism. Some denominations practice it. Others do not. For those who do, a brief survey of John Wesley's position is important.

Recall that Wesley's historical and ecclesiastical context differed from ours. In Anglican England, unlike modern evangelicalism, there was only a small Anabaptist influence. Anglicans baptized almost all infants. Instead of asking, "Why baptize infants?" Anglicans would have asked, "Why not baptize infants?" As an Anglican, Wesley would have agreed. There would have been no reason for rebaptism.

Wesley does not explain infant baptism. Nevertheless, careful study reveals how he differs from his Anglican context. He moved away from the predominately Catholic doctrine that infant baptism cancels the *guilt* of original sin. Rather, according to Wesley, prevenient grace removes guilt if there is any at all.

With reference to practicing infant baptism in the holiness tradition, Rob Staples notes a decline in its practice in the Church of the Nazarene. He explains:

> Powerful arguments have been raised against the doctrine and practice of infant baptism. To many, it seems a scandal because it makes people think they are Christians when they may be nothing of the kind. . . . When we strip away all the verbiage, the arguments against the baptism of infants reduce basically to this: Since as Protestants we believe that salvation is by faith, baptism should be the personal response of our faith to God's grace. Since little children are not old enough to understand the call of God, or to make a conscious choice to respond, they should not be baptized.[14]

This is a thoroughly Anabaptist and, later, a Baptist argument. The problem is that we have no direct theological connection with the Anabaptist or the Baptist traditions. It is erroneous to say Protestants do not baptize children, for many Protestant denominations do. The supposition gains traction among Nazarenes, not because of our theology, but because of an overwhelming rejection of infant baptism by American *evangelicalism*. Because most evangelicals identify themselves by their association with Reformed or Baptist theology, Wesleyans identifying themselves as "evangelicals" is like putting a square peg in a round hole.[15]

Many who *support* infant baptism in the Church of the Nazarene insist we must not violate our Wesleyan DNA. If not, then we must provide solid theological grounding for practicing infant baptism. So, what is it? Answering "Our theology as a whole" is insufficient. Opponents say that because baptism is predicated upon faith, only those old enough to confess faith in Christ are proper candidates for baptism. This objection shifts faith away from the life of the church and toward individuals—a personal transaction only. But this ignores the broader conduits of grace that cultivate faith, especially the church. A report of the Baptism Study Committee of the United Methodist Church explains: "While God is radically free to work in many ways, the church has been given by God the special responsibility and privilege of being the Body of Christ which carries forth God's purposes of redeeming the world. Wesley recognized the church itself as a means of grace."[16] As a "faith-full" community, the church's responsibility is to rear children through discipleship and *their* participation in the (instituted and prudential) means of grace. This is redemption for the child, not in the sense of salvation that comes through a personal experience of new birth, but as a channel for the prevenient grace of God, guiding children toward mature faith. In the process, children are enveloped in and nurtured by the church's faith.

Parents and the church have a responsibility—and faith sufficient—to bring grace to its goal—namely, mature acceptance of Jesus

Christ as Savior. In infant baptism the emphasis *is* on faith—the faith of parents and the body of Christ. In what do they have faith? The reality of God's complete acceptance of the child as a recipient of prevenient grace, God's "wooing grace." This is saving grace. Though we identify various phases or functions of grace—prevenient, saving, and sanctifying grace—God's grace is singular, administered by the Holy Spirit, who offers Christ's benefits to everyone, decisively to those who by grace embrace the faith God offers.

Another way to view infant baptism is that it replaces Jewish circumcision as a sign of the covenant. A Jewish child is not asked whether or not he wants to be circumcised. It happens as an expression of the community's faith, a reality worth celebrating.

We should distinguish infant baptism from infant dedication. The latter focuses on the pledge of the parent(s) to rear a child faithfully. The church supports the parent(s) by pledging to be a surrounding community of faith. While these factors are not absent from infant baptism, the emphasis in the latter unambiguously shifts; infant baptism celebrates God's pledge of commitment to the child and is administered in the name of the Trinity. The liturgical focus is on God as the covenant maker who embraces the child in love and devotion. Infant baptism offers an opportunity for the church to corporately *celebrate* God's prevenient grace as one of our foundational doctrines. Wesley himself wrestled with the "saving" aspect of the sacrament for infants and modified his language over time to emphasize his call for baptized, mature Anglicans to experience new birth.

Second, consider adult baptism. A question is often asked: "If we baptize an infant, are we not denying them opportunity to be baptized later as believers?" Despite our discussion of the corporate faith community, this question is imperative for those who reject infant baptism. It has been answered in two ways. The first option is to *rebaptize* people baptized as infants. This answer is anticreedal and goes against two thousand years of church history. A person can be baptized only once. A second and better option is to reaffirm one's infant baptism. A liturgical opportunity can be provided for a person to stand before the church and reaffirm his or her baptismal faith. Under no conditions should those who have been baptized as adults be rebaptized.

A few concerns remain. *First*, some denominations claim that unless a person is baptized he or she is not saved. We reject this; we believe sacraments are outward signs of inward grace. The act does not save us; it points to the fact that we have been saved and are being saved. *Second*, is baptism in a prior denomination nullified if one joins another denomination? No, not if one's baptism was administered in the name of the Trinity. But if the denomination in question denies the Trinity, then baptism in that setting is not Christian baptism. In this case, a first baptism in the name of the Trinity is necessary. *Third*, does the mode of baptism matter? Some denominations answer that immersion is the only legitimate mode of baptism. We affirm immersion, pouring, and sprinkling of water as acceptable modes of baptism. There must be careful thought in administering both adult and infant baptisms. Allowing the candidate to articulate his or her faith in adult baptism is important. And in both, the person should be baptized in the name of the Trinity.

Administering the Eucharist

Administering the sacraments is not just a matter of practice. It has theological importance as well. Along with the elements, how they are administered is also symbolic.

First, Communion should not be an add-on at the end of a service; it should flow from the sermon or be placed elsewhere with due consideration. A pastor is responsible for meaningfully connecting all parts of a service.

Second, though how we serve Communion is not mandatory, each method makes a theological statement, a sign of a deeper reality. Intinction (usually) requires congregants to move, which can signify an expressed testimony to inward grace received. Intinction also (usually) uses one cup and one loaf, which symbolizes one Lord, and one church that receives him. On the other hand, passing the elements down a row can make us aware of unity with our sisters and brothers. *Who* serves—whether holding the cup and the bread for others or passing the elements from one row to another—is also a theological statement. After the ordained minister institutes (the institution narrative: 1 Cor. 11:23-26; Matt. 26:26-29; Mark 14:22-25; Luke 22:14-20) and consecrates the elements, in the spirit of James 2, we must include and use people from all parts of the body of Christ. Avoid the appearance that only the most powerful are worthy to serve. Include both genders, all ethnicities present, and different ages. Doing so affirms the Protestant principle of the priesthood of all believers.

The liturgy matters. This does not restrict the pastor to the ritual in the *Manual,* but he or she should be very thoughtful about its replacement. An off-the-cuff approach is inappropriate and distracts from the sacrament's sanctity. Two factors are absolutely necessary. *First,* according to the church's tradition, a pastor must acknowledge Christ's institution of the sacrament by reading applicable Scripture. Sacraments were instituted and demanded by our Lord. *Second,* the minister must consecrate the elements, which means to pray they will be a means of grace to recipients. The minister acknowledges the presence of Christ through the Spirit. Be careful to prepare for special needs, such as meeting the needs of those who are gluten free or considering how to provide communion for online communicants.

Conclusion

Sacramental theology and practice are challenging, if not sometimes mystifying. Nevertheless, being a theological steward entails prayerfully and diligently conducting this ministry. It is to be carried out with integrity and in constant recognition of its sanctity and soteriological importance. Stewardship requires nothing less.

Recommended Resources

Felton, Gayle Carlton. *This Holy Mystery: A United Methodist Understanding of Holy Communion*. Nashville: Discipleship Resources, 2005.

Jenson, Robert W. *Visible Words: The Interpretation and Practice of Christian Sacraments*. Minneapolis: Augsburg Fortress, 2010.

Leclerc, Diane, and Mark A. Maddix, eds. *Pastoral Practices: A Wesleyan Paradigm*. Kansas City: Beacon Hill Press of Kansas City, 2013.

Meadows, Philip R. *Remembering Our Baptism: Discipleship and Mission in the Wesleyan Spirit*. Nashville: Discipleship Resources, 2018.

Middendorf, Jesse C. *The Church Rituals Handbook*. 2nd ed. Kansas City: Beacon Hill Press of Kansas City, 2009.

Rattenbury, J. Ernest. *The Eucharistic Hymns of John and Charles Wesley*. Memphis: OSL Publications, 2006.

Staples, Rob L. *Outward Sign and Inward Grace: The Place of Sacraments in Wesleyan Spirituality*. Kansas City: Beacon Hill Press of Kansas City, 1991.

Vickers, Jason E. *A Wesleyan Theology of the Eucharist: The Presence of God for Christian Life and Ministry*. Nashville: General Board of Higher Education and Ministry, 2016.

Wainwright, Geoffrey. *Doxology: The Praise of God in Worship, Doctrine, and Life*. New York: Oxford University Press, 1980. See Wainwright's discussion of infant baptism: 138-42; 328-32.

Wesley, John. "The Duty of Constant Communion." The Sermons of John Wesley—Sermon 101. Wesley Center Online. http://wesley.nnu.edu/john -wesley/the-sermons-of-john-wesley-1872-edition/sermon-101-the-duty -of-constant-communion/.

Wesley, John, and Charles Wesley. *Hymns on the Lord's Supper*. London: J. Kershaw, 1825. Internet Archive. https://archive.org/details/hymnsonlords supp00wesl/page/n5/mode/2up. In addition to hymns on the Lord's Supper, this source is very important for seeing how the Wesleys understood the Eucharist.

8
STEWARD OF PRAYER

Jesse C. Middendorf, DMin

IN THE CHURCH TRADITION in which I serve, ordination of ministers is a holy occasion. A quality of solemnity characterizes the event
in a manner seldom equaled in other settings. One feature of the service is reading pertinent paragraphs from the denomination's govern-
ing *Manual* in which clergy duties are specified. The final paragraph
issues direct and sobering challenges:

> The minister must have gifts and graces, for the ministry. He or
> she will have a thirst for knowledge, especially of the Word of
> God, and must have sound judgment, good understanding, and
> clear views concerning salvation as revealed in the Scriptures.
> Saints will be edified and sinners converted through his or her
> ministry. Further, the minister of the gospel in the Church of the
> Nazarene must be an example in prayer.[1]

The final sentence is almost always emphasized. Its tones ring
in the ears of all who hear, especially the ordinands. It often brings
tears to the eyes of ordained clergy as they recall their ordination.
The paragraph is a straightforward and sobering reminder of what
is expected of Christian ministers. Is it possible to fulfill the charge?
Yes, and prayer is an essential part of the process. It is an essential
ingredient of a Christian minister's lifeblood.

The importance of prayer is demonstrated in the life of Jesus.
There are repeated references to Jesus praying (e.g., Matt. 14:23;
26:36-45; Mark 6:46; Luke 5:16; John 17:1-26). He sought guidance
from his Father, even for deliverance from the impending agony of the
cross (Matt. 26:36-39; Luke 22:39-46). In Luke's Gospel, Jesus told
his disciples a parable to demonstrate they should always pray and
not give up (Luke 18:1-8).

The apostle Paul stressed the importance of praying "without
ceasing" (1 Thess. 5:17, KJV). In several letters he requested prayer
for himself and his companions (e.g., Rom. 15:30-32; 2 Cor. 1:10-11;
1 Thess. 5:25; 2 Thess. 3:1-2).

Prayer as a Way of Life

Just as prayer was essential for Jesus, so it is for ministers of the gospel. Far more than designating a set time of the day, prayer is a pastor's way of *being in the world*. It involves practicing the presence of God. It is foundational for ministry and for our relationship with God.

From the beginning, God desired communion with his creation, especially with humans created to bear God's image. Genesis 3:8 speaks of the Lord "walking in the garden in the cool of the day," seeking Adam and Eve, expecting communion with them. He asked, "Where are you?" (v. 9). This shows that God is graciously disposed toward communion. No one needs to seek God's attention or fear his or her prayers are not good enough. Our gracious God is not distant. He is not occupied with things more important than communion with us. He is nearer than breath itself (Pss. 34:18; 145:18).

Susan and I are in our fifty-sixth year of marriage. Much of the past year has been spent in quarantine, as we have tried to protect ourselves and others against the COVID-19 virus. We are retired. So we have spent these months in close interchange. The time has been very meaningful. But we have missed being with others. We have longed to hold our infant granddaughter, hug our older grandchildren, and spend time with our family. Phone calls and video chats with friends and loved ones have helped. But absent that, months in relative isolation have yielded a renewed appreciation for each other, a deeper intimacy than we have thought possible. We have cherished being together. Our conversations have been rich; our study of Scripture has been rewarding. We have grown even more deeply in love. We can sit in silence and then suddenly continue a conversation that might have begun hours or days before. Often we finish each other's sentences. Communion is a lived reality. None of this means we take each other for granted or overlook seeking the best for each other. We can't neglect the discipline of cultivating our relationship, of cultivating communion.

It is little wonder the apostle Paul sometimes uses the metaphor of marriage for the church and for our relationship with God. The mutuality of love and respect, of serving one another, of caring for the best interests of the other, remind us that it requires work to make a marriage flourish. That is not a hindrance or defect. It simply recognizes relationships require intentional and persistent attention. It entails honest communication, which leads to maturing communion.

If this is true of marriage, how much more is it true of our intimacy with God? Prayer is a requisite part of the atmosphere in which communion with God thrives.

The Disciplines of Prayer

Prayer requires more than aspiring to make communion with God central to Christian ministry. It entails practices that foster communion.

Within the Wesleyan tradition, practicing disciplines that promote communion with God has been normative. This is not unique to Wesleyans. As far back as King David we find prayer being practiced in various forms and settings, characterized by a hunger for intimacy with God. The book of Psalms is the "original" prayer book. The psalmists voice petitions and lament, as well as thanksgiving, adoration, and worship.

Sometimes the psalms reveal agonizing honesty. Their writers did not squelch their frustrations over God's apparent indifference to injustice, illness, loss, and hypocrisy. Nor did they hide their need for confession. Psalm 51 expresses anguish by one who has failed in his covenant responsibilities, is convicted of his sin, and humbly confesses before God. He prays for cleansing, for a clean heart, and commits to changes of comprehensive dimensions.

Such honesty characterizes Wesleyan spirituality. Confessing our need for God's grace and forgiveness must be done fearlessly in the presence of the God whose "steadfast love endures forever" (Ps. 136, RSV). Writing to the Corinthians, the apostle Paul urged them to "examine" themselves, to make sure they were "holding to [their] faith," and recognizing the implications of Christ being "in" them! (2 Cor. 13:5, RSV).

What Paul urges upon the Corinthians is equally true for Christian ministers. A robust prayer life is an essential path to the goal, part of a larger whole. In *The Spirit of the Disciplines* Dallas Willard counsels, "Prayer almost always involves other disciplines and spiritual activities if it is to go well, especially study, meditation, and worship, and often solitude and fasting as well."[2]

No amount of busyness, duties fulfilled, or meetings and conferences attended can supplant the need for prayer to nurture a congregation. They certainly cannot generate an intimacy with God that yields Christlikeness.

As Dallas Willard counseled, prayer must be complemented by other disciplines and spiritual activities. Absorption in the Word of God is central. Otherwise, prayer becomes shallow, an echo chamber. This entails loving and careful study and unhurried meditation or contemplation. Sitting in silence before the Lord, we can cultivate a capacity for discerning the Spirit's voice. Contemplative prayer cultivates communion *with* God, beyond speaking *to* him.

This requires surrender of "our agenda" as primary. In Christian ministry we are often driven by our lists, our schedules, our duties. These things can crowd out listening for the voice of the Lord. Don't misunderstand. This does not require adopting a monastic lifestyle that abandons other responsibilities. The discipline of prayer can thrive amid busy schedules. Henri Nouwen puts it this way:

A life without a quiet center easily becomes delusional. When we cling to the results of our actions as our only way of self-identification, we become possessive, defensive, and dependent on false identities. In the solitude of prayer we slowly unmask the illusion of our dependencies and possessiveness, and discover in the center of our own self that we are not what we can control or conquer but what is given to us from above to channel to others. In solitary prayer we become aware that our identity does not depend on what we have accomplished or possess, that our productivity does not define us, and that our worth is not the same as our usefulness.[3]

Surely Nouwen is correct. Prayer helps form the center from which ministry proceeds.

"Teach Us to Pray"

The disciplines of prayer in a minister's life help form the springboard for teaching God's people. The words "discipline" and "discipleship" come from the same root word. Making Christlike disciples, apprentices, of Jesus is the heart of Christian ministry. We are to lead believers into transforming encounters with the risen Christ. A minister nurtures the body of Christ, models the faith for them, and guides them in the disciplines of Christian faith. Maturation in Christlikeness is his or her goal and reward.

In the Gospel of Luke, one of Jesus's disciples observed Jesus praying. When Jesus finished, the disciple said, "Lord, teach us to pray, just as John taught his disciples" (11:1). Here Luke's account of the Lord's Prayer occurs. The unnamed disciple recognized prayer as foundational for Jesus's life and ministry.

In the Gospel of Matthew (5:1-7:27) we find the Sermon on the Mount—the "constitution of the kingdom of God." Prayer is central for the Sermon. It includes Matthew's account of the Lord's Prayer (6:9-13). It is introduced by instructions for how to pray (vv. 5-8).

Just as Jesus taught his disciples to pray, pastors must teach their congregations how to pray. Pastors are stewards of prayer. Teaching Christian doctrine, how to study the Bible, the meaning of the sacraments, and how Christian holiness is to be lived are all vital pastoral responsibilities. But unless we teach believers to pray, all else will prove shallow and inadequate for facing the challenges of Christian discipleship. To repeat: *Pastors are stewards of prayer!*

We teach first by making prayer central to our own lives. Then hopefully congregants will echo that disciple of long ago: "Pastor, teach us to pray." This will require intentional planning and effort.

Prayer as a way of life is not a solitary activity; it does not happen in a vacuum. The gathered body of Christ becomes the workshop of the Spirit for learning to pray. Pastors are to instruct their people in what John Wesley termed the "means of grace." These are channels through which the Spirit of God conveys grace to God's people. In *Spiritual Formation: A Wesleyan Paradigm*, Diane Leclerc notes,

> Wesley divided the "means of grace" into three divisions: instituted means of grace, the prudential means of grace, and the general means of grace. The *instituted* means of grace are practices given directly by Jesus Christ. They are: prayer, searching the Scriptures, participating in the Lord's Supper (Eucharist), fasting, and Christian conferencing (spiritual conversation). The *prudential* means of grace are practices that are wise and beneficial to do. They include obeying Christ, small groups, special prayer meetings, visiting the sick, doing all the good we can to all the people we can, and reading from the devotional classics of the rich tradition of two thousand years of Christianity. The prudential means of grace were designed to meet the person at his or her point of need, thus they are adaptable to a person's particular historical situation or context. The *general* means of grace include: watching, denying ourselves, taking up our cross daily, and exercising the presence of God.[4]

These means of grace are instructive, but not exhaustive. God's creative grace can work in other ways, as well. Prayer is pivotal for all means of grace

Through the Holy Spirit, the triune God always graciously provides ways for knowing and serving him, never leaving us to only our wits and capacities. But God's provisions always call for response from us. This does not mean our response causes our redemption. Even our obedience is enabled by grace. God's gracious work is never coercive.

For that reason a pastor, as steward, must strive to identify avenues by which God's people can freely respond to their gracious God.

This pastoral responsibility is central for the Wesleyan tradition. John Wesley's classes, bands, and societies provided the framework for much of the eighteenth-century Evangelical Revival in Great Britain. The theological foundations that undergirded the revival were of primary importance. John's instruction and preaching and Charles's hymns helped fuel the revival. But it was sustained by a carefully developed structure that provided pathways along which people, in community, could respond to God's outpouring of grace.

The Pastoral Prayer

Perhaps the most visible expression of our stewardship of prayer occurs in the pastoral prayer. While in some congregations this priestly role has been diminished or even set aside, in the life of the people of God it should remain a vital part of a pastor's ministry.

When Solomon's temple was dedicated (1 Kings 8:1-66; 2 Chron. 6:12-42), the king exercised one of the intended functions of Davidic leadership, that of priest before God for the people of Israel. After completing the massive work of temple construction, the people were ready to transition their allegiance from the tabernacle to the permanent structure. They had worked hard for its construction. The temple would now be the meeting place between God and Israel, and eventually between God and all "peoples of the earth" (1 Kings 8:60; 2 Chron. 6:33).

Solomon's prayer was a pastoral prayer voiced on Israel's behalf. He speaks of the temple's role in worship and leads the people in worship (2 Chron. 6:14-15). He intercedes before God on their behalf (1 Kings 8:54-61; 2 Chron. 6:18-31). He prays that God will "incline" the hearts of the people "to walk in all [God's] ways, and to keep his commandments, his statutes, and his ordinances, which he commanded our fathers" (1 Kings 8:58, RSV). Solomon voices the values and virtues that must characterize the relationship between God and

Israel (vv. 22-31). He spells out the meaning of the covenant made between the God of Abraham, Isaac, and Jacob and God's covenant people. Finally, he prays that God will "maintain [the] cause" of his people (v. 49, RSV).

In his text on pastoral theology, Thomas Oden speaks of the pastor's role in public prayer:

> According to most Protestant interpretations of priesthood, the minister is no longer an offerer of sacrifice to God according to the Levitical pattern, because that has already adequately occurred in Jesus Christ. So what remains for the Christian minister to do in the priestly office? The Christian minister representatively intercedes on behalf of the faithful community before God in prayer as a timely, public, verbal, hearable act.[5]

Oden has made clear the irreplaceable role the pastoral prayer plays in a pastor's responsibility for the care of souls. Fulfilling this distinct privilege must flow from a pastor's deep communion with God as he or she prepares for the gathering of the people for worship. This requires far more than a prayer list and a stream of extemporaneous sentences. The pastoral prayer requires careful thought, planning, and direction.

It will also require a deep relationship with one's congregants—their successes and failures, their aspirations and needs. If the pastoral prayer evidences a pastor's communion with God and a comprehensive love for people, if it reflects a pastor's breadth of joy and acquaintance with the needs carried by those gathered for worship, then the Holy Spirit can apply the prayer to those present. His or her prayer becomes a means of grace. In the power of the Holy Spirit, a pastor gathers up the prayers of the people and offers them to their listening God in worship, petition, intercession, and thanksgiving. He or she voices a corporate and individual hunger for God.

Requiring careful thought, a pastoral prayer should not tax a congregation's endurance. The traditional fourfold structure of prayer can serve as a model.

First, Adoration

Praise and adoration form the foundation for all prayer, especially pastoral prayers. God alone is worthy of adoration and worship. By gracious invitation we worship the triune God as Creator, Redeemer, giver of "every good and perfect gift" (James 1:17), healer of our diseases, and sovereign sustainer of his world. Adoration arises because of who God is and because in our poverty of spirit he invites us into his presence as his beloved children.

Second, Petition

Here Christians are at their most vulnerable. We come before God, not because of our worthiness, but because we are desperately in need of God's mercy. We make no presumptions about an audience with God. We confess our need for his gracious attention. A wise pastor recognizes and articulates a congregation's need for God's forgiveness—corporately and individually. He or she states clearly that God's grace makes confession both necessary and possible. No one, no matter how saintly, stands above the need for honest confession. Jesus's parable of the Pharisee and the tax collector makes this clear (Luke 18:9-14). The tax collector "went home justified before God" (v. 14). As Christians growing in Christlikeness, redeemed and being redeemed (Phil. 1:6; 2:12-13), we confidently confess our numberless infirmities to the Lord. Contrary to what some might think, confession expresses confidence, not its deficit, in our transforming God (1 John 1:5-10). Love casts out all fear of honesty before God (4:18).

Third, Intercession

Interceding before God for the needs and hopes of a congregation is a central component. Here the everyday stresses of life, the "diseases" that infiltrate our families, workplaces, neighborhoods, and world, are brought before our heavenly Father. A pastor *represents* petitions; he or she does not *expose* individual needs. A pastor's intercession before God assures God's people that they are not alone in their struggles. God is already intimately acquainted with them.

Intercessory prayer teaches by expanding a congregation's range of interest in and consciousness of the wide reach of God's kingdom. Intercession includes individual interest. But it must go much further to include, for example, prayer for those who do not know Christ, for God's mission in all the earth, for missionaries, for the persecuted church, and for social justice. Unless intercession reaches beyond personal needs, believers might not live out Paul's instruction that "supplications, prayers, intercessions, and thanksgivings be made for all men. . . . This is good, and it is acceptable in the sight of God our Savior, who desires all men to be saved and to come to the knowledge of the truth" (1 Tim. 2:1-4, RSV).

Fourth, Thanksgiving

Here the pastoral prayer reaches its summit in full-throated gratitude. We have prayed! God has listened! There has been communion with God. Grace has been and will continue to be operative.

By beginning pastoral prayer with adoration, we affirmed that by grace our holy God is accessible. By concluding our prayer in thanksgiving, we affirm that our God is love. These are the bookends that provide context for petition and intercession.

Recall that a pastoral prayer models prayer for a congregation; it helps shape the practices of our people. It demonstrates the meaning of prayer in the Christian journey. In his book *Thinking, Listening, Being: A Wesleyan Pastoral Theology*, Jeren Rowell observes, "Pastors praying in the worshipping community of faith and leading the congregation in prayer is certainly important, but [there] is also a dangerous temptation to pray impressively, passionately, or manipulatively. . . . The challenge is to avoid simply praying *for* the people but rather to lead the people in praying."[6]

Being a pastor is a gift of God's grace, and so is the pastoral prayer.

Conclusion

If people to whom we minister are to be formed according to the gospel of Jesus Christ and shaped for ministry in the world, then our stewardship of prayer—for ourselves and for others—must be passionately observed. Otherwise, in-depth discipleship will not occur, no matter how much Bible study we and our people practice. Our teaching is partly predicated upon our own learning and practice. Together, as Christ's body, we learn to hear, delight in, and respond to the voice of the Lord, who names us his beloved.

Recommended Resources

Bible, Ken. *Nurturing Your Creativity and Your Life in Christ.* KenBible.com. Accessed March 15, 2022. https://kenbible.com.

Bloesch, Donald G. *The Struggle of Prayer.* Colorado Springs: Helmers and Howard, 1988.

Leclerc, Diane, and Mark Maddix, eds. *Spiritual Formation: A Wesleyan Paradigm.* Kansas City: Beacon Hill Press of Kansas City, 2011.

LNWhymns.com. Accessed March 15, 2022. https://lnwhymns.com/Default .aspx.

Oden, Thomas C. *Pastoral Theology: Essentials of Ministry.* San Francisco: Harper and Row, 1983.

Spurgeon, Charles H. *The Pastor in Prayer.* N.p.: Fig, 2012.

Truesdale, Al, ed. *The Book of Saints.* 5 vols. Kansas City: Beacon Hill Press of Kansas City, 2013–18.

———. *When You Can't Pray: Finding Hope When You're Not Experiencing God.* 2nd ed. Kansas City: Beacon Hill Press of Kansas City, 2016.

Willard, Dallas. *The Divine Conspiracy: Rediscovering Our Hidden Life in God.* San Francisco: HarperSanFrancisco, 1998.

9
STEWARD OF THE BIBLICAL MORAL VISION

Timothy M. Green, PhD

AFTER ENTERING PASTORAL MINISTRY, I soon realized I often shared as little as two hours each week with most of the flock entrusted to my care. As congregants departed worship services, Bible studies, church fellowships, committee meetings, and counseling sessions, they returned to their homes, workplaces, schools, and other activities. There they encountered the question faced by the people of God throughout history: "How are we to know and do what is appropriate—*good*—in the eyes of God?"

So where do our people turn for an answer to this compelling question? To their preferred website or news source? To their favorite author or blogger? To a political or social entity with which they share a kindred spirit or common agenda? While the sources to which Christians may turn are plentiful, as pastors we recognize we have been called to and entrusted with the sacred Scriptures and tasked with embodying them in word and deed as they bear witness to God.

How We Enter Scripture Matters

Although turning to Scripture seems to be a pastoral given, one of the most challenging things we face is *how* to faithfully help our people *enter Scripture*.[1] Imagine with me a common scenario. A question comes up about the *good* of God as related to a specific topic. In response, we almost naturally search for the most relevant biblical passages related to the topic. While omitting some passages, we select others and merge them into a single answer or series of bullet points. We then conclude that we have adequately provided a biblical answer.

This well-intentioned process presents an unintentional double-edged sword. On the one hand, as a few selected lines are lifted from the whole of Scripture, we inadvertently reduce the Bible to a cut-and-paste sourcebook of disconnected proof texts or propositions on what "to do" or what "not to do" in diverse situations.[2] Severed from the larger biblical narrative, our sourcebook can be shaped into our own image or into the image of our affinity group. As a result, the Bible functions more as an idol for domesticating God or managing people than it does as a witness to God's character and activity.

On the other hand, out of a well-intended goal of addressing a specific topic—perhaps the hot topic of the day—the piecemeal strategy fails to draw upon the grand narrative of Scripture, which should become the starting point for forming our vision of the *good* of God. Although we know that who we *are* and what we *do* should emerge from who God *is* and what God *does*, hot topics can subtly supplant the centrality of God in the formation of our people. Stanley Hauerwas and William Willimon have correctly observed that "we are forever getting confused into thinking that scripture is mainly about what *we* are supposed to do rather than a picture of who God *is*."[3]

When Scripture becomes simply a validating device for dealing with hot topics, Christians can easily begin to identify themselves more as a like-minded social group, shaped by a handful of popular opinions, supplemented with validating biblical proof texts, than they can as a community shaped by the character of God to whom the Scriptures bear witness.

Candidly, throughout my ministry, taking an easy shortcut to the *good* of God has been alluring. The temptation has been to wait for popular issues to emerge and then lift a handful of passages out of the Bible to address the topics. However, deep in my pastoral heart I have known that Christian ministers are called to "correctly [handle] the word of truth" (2 Tim. 2:15) in a manner that invites laypersons into a deeper and wider transformation informed by the grand narrative of Scripture. Biblical footnotes used to address hot topics will never achieve this.

I also know by God's grace that what is *good* in the eyes of my people can be "re-formed" to comply with what is *good* in the eyes of God. Out of fidelity to my congregants and to the Scriptures, I could and would not settle for an inferior assessment of the *good* of God.

Pastoring within a Biblical Moral Vision

How might we, as Christian ministers, move beyond applying biblical texts in a piecemeal manner to address popular topics? As theological stewards who believe Scripture "is useful for teaching, rebuking, correcting and training in righteousness" (2 Tim. 3:16), how might we faithfully minister from *within* the Bible's grand narrative? As pastor—and congregants—we must be formed by the Bible's interwoven and embedded moral vision of the *good* of God. Rather than imposing on Scripture our own perceptions of what is good, we must permit the *good* of God to emerge *from* Scripture.

Defining Moral Vision

To understand what is meant by moral vision, we will begin by thinking about the phrase "*good* in the eyes of . . ." Through the metaphor of eyes, we describe how one sees or views, perceives or understands. Based upon how we see or understand something to be good, we proceed to make decisions and act upon them. Hauerwas and Willimon remind us that "we can only act within a world we can see. Vision is the necessary prerequisite for ethics."[4] Simply stated, moral vision is how we see or understand what is *good*.

A community's shared moral vision does not appear out of thin air. It is predominantly shaped by and embedded within a grand narrative that characterizes a community. But as pastors we often unexpectedly discover additional underlying narratives shaping our congregants' perceptions of what is ultimately good. These may emerge from family, culture, childhood influence, dispositions or even one's nation. Often we are so deeply enculturated that we are not aware of the subsidiary moral visions in play.

As stewards of the biblical moral vision, it is imperative that from time to time we pause to ask, What is our vision of what is ultimately *good*, and how did it arise?

From the grand narrative of Scripture, it is possible to articulate a biblical moral vision by employing a range of images such as love, fidelity, holiness, community, and kingdom of God. While recognizing the importance of each of these, we need to remember there is a more comprehensive moral vision from which discreet images emerge. It is composed, as taught in Scripture, of all God is doing in the world and of *how* God is doing it. The central and uniting image is *covenant.*[5]

The Meaning and Place of Covenant in the Life of God's People

To conceive what it might mean for congregants to be formed *from within* the biblical vision of covenant, we must grasp its meaning and theological importance in Scripture. While the ancient world described mutually binding relationships between two or more parties in terms of covenant, our biblical ancestors used the term to describe the Lord inviting them into a mutually committed and binding relationship.

God initiated a series of covenants, the first being God's covenant with creation in which God pledged to Noah that he would preserve the stability of nature (Gen. 9:8-17). This was followed by the covenant with Abraham. God promised Abraham and Sarah the blessing of land and descendants. They were to become God's blessing to the world (17:1-22). Later the Lord established a covenant with David, promising a dynasty in which David's descendants would succeed him on the throne (2 Sam. 7:1-17).[6]

Rather than a covenant coming to an end or being annulled by subsequent covenants, each one successively builds upon another. Through covenant making, God portrays his consistent relational character. Ultimately, the covenants were intended for the whole world.

While each covenant has a significant role, the Lord's covenant with the Hebrew people at Sinai was pivotal (Exod. 19:1-6). The mutually relational quality of the Sinai covenant repeats throughout Scripture in the phrase "I will be your God, and you will be my people." Centuries later, as the exiled community questioned whether

God had abandoned the Sinai covenant and his people, Jeremiah saw a day on the horizon when the Lord would create a new covenant. Through it divine instruction (*torah*) would be inscribed on the community's mind rather than on stone tablets. The new covenant would continue the relational quality of the Sinai covenant. "I will be their God, and they will be my people" (Jer. 31:33).

As the biblical narrative unfolds, the early Christian church believed the new covenant is established as believers participate in the broken body and shed blood of Jesus Christ (Luke 22:17-20; 1 Cor. 11:23-26). With hope-filled anticipation, participants in this new covenant await the consummation of God's kingdom, including new creation, when "they will be his people, and God himself will be with them and be their God" (Rev. 21:3).

Creation as the "Sphere" in Which Covenant Takes Place[7]

Although the word "covenant" does not appear until after the flood, from the opening lines of Genesis we encounter the essence of God's nature embodied in covenant: mutual relationality that wills to create mutual relationship with the creation. Terence Fretheim observes, "God has taken the initiative and freely entered into relationships, both in creation and in covenant with Israel. But, having done so, God—who is other than world—has decisively and irrevocably committed the divine self to be in a *faithful relationship.*"[8]

With God's first communication in Scripture, "Let there be" (Gen. 1:3), God makes space for the *other,* for the creation, and fills it with "a reality distinct from God."[9] Then God enters mutual relationship with the *other.*[10] In this Creator-creature relationship, God relates to humans as an authentic "you" with whom to share a mutual relationship.[11] This reveals God's essential relational character (who God is) and what God will consistently commit to doing. This binding mutual I-You relationship becomes the premise for all that will unfold as God opens himself to the *other* in covenant.

Not only does the Creator intend mutuality with humans, but with all other creatures so that an intricate web of mutuality emerges.[12] When describing this "spider web of a world" in which "interrelatedness is basic to this community of God's creatures," Fretheim notes that "each created entity is in symbiotic relationship with every other and in such a way that any act reverberates out and affects the whole."[13] The apostle Paul's language about the body of Christ describes this interrelationship. "If one part suffers, every part suffers with it; if one part is honored, every part rejoices with it" (1 Cor. 12:26).

God doesn't relate to humans as passive bystanders to be manipulated. Instead, God calls and empowers them to become participants in a life-giving relationship. Instead of mistrust, God makes a "free, gracious commitment and invitation . . . full trust rather than . . . obligation."[14] This intricate web of mutual relationality is *good* in the eyes of God. God repeatedly declares the creation to be *good* (Gen. 1:10, 12, 18, 21, 25, 31).

The Unraveling Web

The world in which our people live shows little resemblance to the *good* of God as the Scriptures reveal it. Enlightened by the Spirit, they observe the distortion and corruption of God's *good* created web of relationship. What people see as *good* in their own eyes supplants what is *good* in the eyes of God (Gen. 3:22; 6:5; 8:21; Isa. 5:20; Rom. 1:18-32).

Like Adam and Eve, out of mistrust and shame, humans hide from the true source of their existence. As a result, gender dominates gender, sibling murders sibling, murderers become fugitives, aliens from the land and strangers in God's presence. Life-taking revenge and violent bloodshed become the norm. The land cries out. Trust and interdependence within the relational web mutates into mistrust and isolation.

In spite of the unraveling, God does not give up. Refusing to circumvent or manipulate humans—the *other*—God remains committed. The Creator continues intricate web building by way of covenant. "I will be your God, and you will be my people." In that covenant, definitively manifest and sealed in the broken body and shed blood of Jesus Christ, our ministry and our people find their identity and their moral vision. The new covenant created in Christ provides God's people with "the gift of hope, the reality of identity, the possibility of belonging, the certitude of vocation."[15]

Envisioning and Living into the Covenantal Form of Life in the Church

Covenant is much more than a contract God "makes" with the church and then files it away in heaven. The covenant's moral vision must become a shared form of life into which God invites the church. How might we as pastors foster in our churches the *good* of God as revealed in the new covenant?

As noted, the essence of a biblical covenant is an intricate web of relationship between God and his creation. It embodies the relational nature of the God we worship. So that Christians may increasingly become like the God they worship, as stewards of the new covenant, pastors must seek to foster congruity between corporate worship and our holy God who calls the church into covenantal life.

As Christians engage in covenant life together, God and one's neighbor are inseparably joined. The commandments to love God (Deut. 6:5) and one's neighbor (Lev. 19:18) emerge in the context of covenant. Within the church's covenantal life, these commands are interwoven. "Anyone who loves God must also love their brother and sister" (1 John 4:21). The same can be said of forgiveness. God's forgiveness of us and our forgiveness of our neighbor are inseparable (Matt. 6:12, 14-15). Likewise, our offerings at the altar are null and void unless there is reconciliation with our neighbor (5:21-26).

Covenant participants are so conjoined that they function as one body. Indeed, "If one part suffers, every part suffers with it; if one part is honored, every part rejoices with it" (1 Cor. 12:26). No member can live in isolation, only in relationship. God's *good* web of relationality contradicts the "heroic good life" of individualistic, privatized religion. This popular notion is fiction. John Wesley insisted there is no "solitary religion," for "the gospel of Christ knows of no religion but social; no holiness but social holiness."[16] The nature of the church is inviolable covenant—with God and fellow Christians.

Interdependence in the body of Christ provides the essential marker for the moral vision associated with covenant. Without it the web unravels and the body dies. The essential marker is *hesed*.[17] Bible translations just don't know what to do with this Hebrew word. Possible translations seem endless: "loving devotion," "faithfulness," "loving-kindness," "unfailing love," "mercy," "steadfast love," "faithful love," or "gracious love" (cf. Lam. 3:22-23). Despite the diversity, the essence of *hesed* is "embodied covenant faithfulness."

Bernhard Anderson says *hesed* arises "from [within] the relationship itself, not from external law or social custom."[18] Apart from a covenant relationship there is no *hesed*. Once a covenant relationship exists, it becomes the covenant's most essential factor. *Hesed* entails faithfulness as essential for a relationship. It refutes the popular notion that freedom necessitates license to move as a consumer from one relationship or community to another. By contrast, a biblical covenant is never about one's individual freedoms; it is always about one's life lived for the sake of the *other*.

Hesed emanates from the character of God. It never gives up, never forsakes, and never abandons the *other*. It always endures to the end. When it seemed God was ready to abandon covenant, the prophet Hosea spoke the unimaginable: "How can I give you up? My heart has changed within me, because I am God and not a human. I am the holy one among you" (Hos. 11:8-9, author's paraphrase). While some may judge the covenant-making God to be weak and naïve, the Bible celebrates God as holy love (Pss. 118:1-29; 136:1-3; Lam. 3:22-23).

Shaped by the Lord's *hesed*, God's people are called to embody the same holy *hesed* and to evidence it toward God and neighbor. In those instances in which a covenant member pulls away from the community, or a member has been cast out by the community, the *hesed* that God extends to his people must be offered to the alienated.

In a covenant relationship each member shares an I-You relationship. John Wesley described the relationship as "in itself generous and disinterested; springing from no view of advantage . . . from no regard to profit or praise."[19] No covenant member can be objectified as an "it" to be manipulated and commodified. Refusing to live by the transactional routine of "I'll scratch your back, if you scratch mine" or "What have you done for me lately?" covenant life proceeds from mutual trust in and respect for the *other*. It proceeds from gratitude for shared life in an authentic I-You community.

To this point, our attention has focused on members *within* the intricate web of covenant. However, for covenant to be true to the character of God, the covenant community—the church—must be porous in its redemptive love for those who are not members of the Christian community. Life within the church must spill out to reach *all* humans, *all* communities, *all* nations, and *all* creation. This is its faithfulness to the character and mission of God.

Therefore, the covenant people who live out the divine *good* of loving their neighbor as they love themselves (Lev. 19:18b) expand that vision (only sixteen verses later) to loving the foreign sojourners as themselves (v. 34). That vision continues to spill out further as the community recognizes the foreigner actually *is* my neighbor (in this case, the Samaritan in Luke 10:25-37). This porous web of relationality spreads even further beyond neighbor and foreigner until it reaches one's enemies (Matt. 5:43-48). From the beginning, covenant was not made for the covenant God and covenant people alone; it was made for the sake of God's *good* for all creation (Gen. 12:3b; Matt. 28:18-20; Gal. 3:7-9; Rev. 7:9-11).

Covenant as Hope-Filled Moral Vision

We have considered what the *good* of God as seen from the perspective of covenant will look like in the church's life. Let's return to the covenant as embedded in the ongoing creative work of God as we are participants in his work of new creation. Born in the heart of the Creator, who is wholly invested in relationship, new creation is central to God's plan. As God's partners we participate in the moral vision entailed by new creation—our unparalleled Christian hope (Rom. 8:20-21; Eph. 4:4; 1 Tim. 4:10). We live in and by resurrection hope embodied in the broken body and shed blood of Jesus Christ. The risen Christ announced, "I am making everything new! . . . It is done. I am the Alpha and the Omega, the Beginning and the End. . . . Those who are victorious will inherit all this, and *I will be their God and they will be my children*" (Rev. 21:5-7; emphasis added).

Conclusion

As stewards of the biblical moral vision, let us as pastors correctly instruct our congregations in the grand moral vision of the Scriptures. Let us help them understand and embrace all the moral contours of covenant. As they occupy their homes and workplaces, as they rear and educate their children, let us be prepared to help answer the perennial question, What is the *good* of God? In one broad stroke the Lord has vividly expressed the biblical moral vision associated with covenant. "He has shown you, O mortal, what is *good*. And what does the LORD require of you? To act justly and to love [*hesed*] and to walk humbly with your God" (Mic. 6:8; emphasis added).

Recommended Resources

Anderson, Bernhard W. *Contours of Old Testament Theology*. Minneapolis: Fortress Press, 1999.

Dunning, H. Ray. *Reflecting the Divine Image: Christian Ethics in Wesleyan Perspective*. Downers Grove, IL: InterVarsity Press, 1998.

Gaines, Timothy R. *Christian Ethics*. Kansas City: Foundry, 2021.

Hauerwas, Stanley, and William H. Willimon. *Resident Aliens: Life in the Christian Colony*. Nashville: Abingdon Press, 1989.

Hays, Richard B. *The Moral Vision of the New Testament: Community, Cross, New Creation: A Contemporary Introduction to New Testament Ethics*. San Francisco: HarperSanFrancisco, 1996.

Meeks, Wayne A. *The Moral World of the First Christians*. Philadelphia: Westminster Press, 1986.

10
STEWARD OF THE CHRISTIAN YEAR

Deirdre R. Brower-Latz, PhD

IF I HAD A POUND (or dollar) for every conversation I have had about someone's busyness, I'd be either very heavy or very rich, depending on my location. The relentless press of demands means time rushes past and my days vanish quickly. Before I know it, a new month is here and I'm left worrying about all I have left to do. When chatting with clergy friends, exhaustion is one of our recurring themes. In a culture of busyness, ingredients are in place for pastors to become absorbed in the unforgiving rush of the world. Too easily, a full schedule becomes the measure of a pastor's value.

That is a temptation we must resist! Our worth is based on how we receive and give God's love. Our lives are valued best in our "interruptibility," the times we pause to meet a stranger's eyes or when we kneel to converse with a child. The model of time we observe in Jesus's life has baked-in moments when it becomes clear that encounters between God and humans proceed by an *alternate rhythm*.

I have begun with time, when discussing the Christian year, because until we realize that we have been sucked into our culture's view of time, we will not see that the pastoral *stewardship of the Christian year* offers a vibrant, deep, positive, and hopeful counteroffer of time for Christians.

Time viewed from the perspective of the Christian year invites Christians into an alternate set of values—namely, the Christian meaning of time and its purpose. We are invited to drink from a pure river that flows in its own direction.

What Is the Christian Year?

Unlike ordinary time, the Christian year is not a calendar year or a set of easily counted days. Instead, it has a rhythm that calls us into the story of God—what Dorothy Sayers called "the most exciting drama that ever staggered the imagination of man."[1] The Christian year offers a range of spaces and ways to meet God on God's terms instead of our own.

In the history and tradition of the church, the yearly Christian rhythm assumes different patterns in various parts of the church. The pattern we will consider is characteristic of the Western church.

A new church year starts with Advent, celebrates the wonderful high day of Christmas, anticipates and then rejoices at Epiphany, shifts into the meditative spaces of Lent, prepares for Easter, and rejoices in the resurrection. The year then moves toward Pentecost and the outpouring of the Holy Spirit. By the Spirit, that inaugural event is recalled and relived here and now. From Pentecost we plunge into "ordinary" time, in which mundane life is carried on and blessed by God's presence. The "ordinary" lives we lead are shaped by the disciplines of prayer, encountering Scripture, and engaging in acts of mercy. The Christian year culminates on Christ the King Sunday, when Christians celebrate Christ as King of kings and Lord of all. The entire year has led to this grand affirmation.

Why We Observe the Christian Year

Later we will examine how the Christian year can shape discipleship, for that is what it is all about. But first let's consider why we observe the Christian calendar. Why do Christians shape the year so different from secular time? This requires examining the theology of time.

What do we know about time? This might seem obvious, but not so. In Genesis 1:3-5, we hear that God created time—daytime and nighttime, wake time and sleep time. A pattern for the week is woven into creation. It involves production and fruitful activity, friendship making, companionship, conversation, walking with God, and sleep and rest. So humankind's beginning is closely associated with time and eternity. When considered, from God's perspective, time assumes unique importance.

Recall that Jesus came *in time* (Luke 2:6-7; Gal. 4:4). His birth within a culture is important for our understanding of time. Jesus was a faithful Jew. He interpreted and sometimes reinterpreted the law. He conversed with others in diverse settings—during meals, at parties, while rowing and fishing, and so on. He spoke good news to crowds and individuals. He was immersed in his world and that of others.

The basis for observing the Christian year, and pastoral stewardship of it, is that the Gospels lead us through Jesus's life story. We witness redemption unfolding, new creation being born step-by-step, event-by-event, as the Father procures salvation for the world through his Son. We are gifted witnesses and are changed by the unfolding of the story.

God created time and redemptively shapes it for humans. There are Sabbaths, times for pausing from work. Eugene Peterson noted that according to Scripture, pausing for the Sabbath is an act of defiance and a declaration.[2] Keeping time and setting time aside for God are part of our call as leaders. From *this* place, we serve.

Who *cannot* rest on the Sabbath? Hebrew slaves in Egypt making bricks. Who *cannot* rest on the Sabbath? Hebrew slaves being forced to work. Who could but does not pause? A greedy and rapacious merchant. Who *can* rest? God's people, delivered from slavery, learning that when worshipping God, the whole creation can rest. At rest, they tell and show what God is like through storytelling and through Sabbath feasting with family and guests. They recall that while sleeping, God is carrying them. When the Sabbath arrives, they gather for worship to sing, pray, and remember that Yahweh is the one who constitutes them a people and who is redemptively in their midst. These holy rhythms of time shaped the Hebrews and their community.

The Jewish Christians who first formed the church carried forward the Jewish rhythms of time. They gathered to tell the story of Jesus—the life, death, resurrection, and ascension of their Lord. They ate and worshipped together. They sang hymns to their *Kyrios* (Phil. 2:5-11; Col. 1:15-20; 1 Tim. 3:16; Heb. 1:1-3; 1 Pet. 2:21-25). As a distinctive community of the "Jesus way," they marked time according to the Jesus story. What the early Christians initiated, the church in subsequent times continued and enriched as constitutive of their identity.

Obviously our secular world isn't shaped that way. We live in a nonstop world where the economy is always running. Often those least paid can't stop, while the highest paid are on overdrive and won't stop. For many, work becomes life's significance. This observation is meant to describe, not to induce guilt in the lives of Christians.

We should now be able to see that for Christians, time should primarily be understood with reference to the kingdom of God. Fundamentally, a Christian understanding of time should be formed according to the story of our Redeemer, even though we, too, live in a secular world that shapes time in other ways. Historically, this has been true for the church.

Let's move a step further. As Christians, our lives are gifted. They are also God's gift to the world. As Easter people we are to live as though heaven is touching earth now—where we live and have our being. N. T. Wright observes that because of Jesus's victory, "a new reality has come to birth."[3] Now, the value of time is seasoned by the salt of Easter faith and by expecting the kingdom's consummation. So for Christians time is precious in a way not characteristic of secular time. Time understood and used in a Christian way serves God's kingdom and other people.

Like a "thief in the night," a Christian understanding of time can be stolen from us. We can become so busy that we do not realize the thief is at work. Stewardship of the Christian year, of a Christian understanding of time, can thwart the thief.

As Christ followers, God's time is operative in us. We are carriers of God's time and of his plans for his world. Eternity is making itself at home in us. That is why we observe the Christian year. Pastors are its chief stewards in Christ's church.

The Christian Year Shapes Discipleship

The beauty of the Christian year is that it holds to an alternate pattern. When we are shaped by it, it molds us into thinking differently. Gone is December as a "shop 'til you drop" month. Instead, we meditate on hope, peace, joy, and love, often through the characters of the Bible such as the light bearers, the prophets, John the Baptist, and Mary, or on biblical Christmas themes. We anticipate Jesus's birth. But instead of wrapping it in paper topped with chintzy bows (nothing wrong with gifts), we ask, "How is God preparing us to receive the Christ child anew?" Or "What prophetic witness will help us understand how God's promises have been fulfilled?" We consider how we display Christian hope in dark times or faith amid a doubting world.

When we have spent time during Advent reflecting on how the Father sent his Son to be light for a darkened world, and after we have considered humble and obedient Mary and Joseph, it is time to consider Jesus's incarnation, Immanuel, "God with us." A congregation's consideration of the incarnation is vital. What was true of Christ's birth so many centuries ago is true now: God is for us!

Christmas brings with it a call to commitment and transformation. John Wesley's Covenant Renewal Service[4] often occurred during the Christmas season as a time for reflecting upon and renewing commitment to God's will. This punctuation of the Christian year emphasized sacrifice, sending, going, and being. Hearing each other share a prayer of covenant, invoking God's help to follow beside each other, is a powerful affirmation.

So Christmas takes us into the space of revelation. We are reminded that worldly power hates and seeks to destroy the infant. The empire wants to suffocate competition to its boast of power.

Epiphany—learning how God reveals his glory and redemption to the world—follows Christmas. We examine how we see God at work and in whom (Matt. 2:1-6). We again consider God, the revealer of himself, teaching us and finding ways to open our eyes. We can reconsider our baptism, Jesus's miracles, the "I am" sayings in John's Gospel[5] that tell us who Jesus is, and the great joy Jesus brings to our lives.

After Epiphany we move into "ordinary" time, or a space between. These are the numbered days between Epiphany and Lent and, later, between Pentecost and Christ the King Sunday. They take up most of the Christian year and occupy the periods that fall outside the major seasons. Ordinary time represents the ordered life of the church. It can be thought of as a fallow time, a time for watchfulness and expectation.

Ash Wednesday prepares us for the season of Lent. The imposition of ashes on our foreheads is deeply humbling. It reminds us we are mortals and prepares us to enter the season of Lent. We hear the words spoken, "Remember that 'dust thou art, and unto dust shalt thou return' [Gen. 3:19, KJV]." But we are also forgiven and live in hope of the resurrection.

Lent launches us into forty days of self-examination and self-denial, repentance, prayer, fasting, contemplation, and hopeful preparation. As we follow Jesus to Jerusalem and to the cross, we are reminded that as Christians we are cross-formed people. Suffering with our Lord is essential for discipleship.

Some of the ways I practice Lent is to eat frugally and give what remains to a homeless shelter. I remove one item a day from my home and box it up for a charity shop. Others fast from food, Twitter, TV, or email during part of the day. Some people write a prayer of gratitude each day. The point is that during Lent we craft a habit of carefully considering God in our everyday life. We remember that there is a time to mourn, to weep, to reflect, to be still—all for considering Jesus in special ways.

From Lent we move into Passion Week. Passion Week begins with Palm Sunday and continues through the remembrance of the Last Supper (or Maundy Thursday) and Good Friday (or Black Friday) and culminates with the highest celebration in the Christian calendar: Easter.

Stewarding the spaces of lament, temptation, wilderness, and suffering is important for pastors. Often we hold people's fragility, suffering, and pain. Part of our role as pastor is to assure people their vulnerabilities are contained by God's love.

Easter season lingers. It is a *time*, not simply one day. We celebrate and reemphasize Easter for fifty days, reaffirming that "Christ is risen" and that his cross and resurrection inaugurate the new creation. We call our congregation to live confidently in the Christian hope of resurrection and our Lord's return.

From Easter we lean into Pentecost. The outpouring of the Spirit is celebrated, the birth of the church, and the creation of the new people of God.

Pentecost is followed by the second period of ordinary time. Most of the church year is "ordinary." In ordinary time we welcome the presence of the sanctifying Spirit into the ordinary dimensions of our lives. Christian holiness is lived out in real life. Light and salt bearing are good symbols for ordinary time.

Next comes Christ the King Sunday.[6] By the Holy Spirit we commit to living lives through which the Holy Spirit can bring the full reign of Christ to completion in all creation. On this day many Christians sing Charles Wesley's hymn "Rejoice, the Lord Is King" (1744).

> *[Christ's] kingdom cannot fail;*
> *He rules o'er earth and heav'n.*
> *The keys of death and hell*
> *Are to our Jesus giv'n.*
> *Lift up your heart; lift up your voice!*
> *Rejoice; again I say, rejoice.*

What the Christian Year Provides for Pastors

First, the Christian year provides opportunity for *intentional discipleship* based upon the life of Jesus. Year after year, we follow Jesus from his birth to his ascension. This provides a progressive encounter with him, an opportunity to relive the course of his ministry. This helps Christians to deepen their faith and to place themselves in the story of God.

Second, by observing the progression of the Christian year, believers are reminded they are equal members of the body of Christ. Unlike the secular environment, the rhythms of the Christian year remind us that in Christ there are no rich and poor, healthy and ill, young and old, or any other form of division. In Christ, and by the Spirit, the Father has created one new and true humanity (Eph. 2:14-16). Because we are in Christ, we are united with one another in Christ, who is our head. Our lives together are framed by a new meaning, as lived and explained throughout the Christian year; together we relive the Christian meaning of time.

Third, events of the Christian year can prepare us for worship, for it encloses the full range of revelation and redemption. It includes the sweep of life and emotions. Parts of the year can guide a pastor as he or she exhorts and equips congregations to live lives that bear witness to God's presence in all of life. Throughout the year, hard questions of sin, destruction, oppression, forgiveness, redemption, and other such issues can be addressed. A pastor leads his or her people to relearn the Bible. Its stories, genealogies, sacred history, poetry, prophecies, Gospels, Epistles, and apocalyptic writings—all are found in the Christian year. The Bible teaches throughout the year.

Fourth, related to the third reason, the rhythm of the Christian year provides a platform for planning services of worship and nourishing discipleship. It recalls our whole lived experience and rehearses God's loving actions in the world. It keeps us from isolating ourselves against the world, for it relives the story of God's love *for* the world. The rhythms of the Christian year teach us that God's mission is our mission—in all spaces and places.

Fifth, the Christian year offers a pastor opportunity to teach Christian doctrine, to show that faith consists of the entire story of God with us. That story enables us to confront difficult questions about God, about oppression and injustice, redemption and liberation, sin and evil, and forgiveness and hope. Christians are equipped to bear witness to God's transforming grace in a broken world. All this forces a pastor throughout the year prayerfully to reflect on God's ways and to listen for God's voice.

Sixth, the Christian way of marking time counters secular practices that reduce Christian holy days to selfish consumption. It takes our eyes, hands, and wallets off of *holidays* and reclaims them as *holy days*, as formational times and places for encountering and being encountered by God. It is a way to remind God's people that all their days are holy days, for they are being formed by the love of God, who gave his only Son that the world might be redeemed, made a new creation.

Seventh, the Christian calendar provides a pattern for preaching that ensures the whole sweep of Scripture and the gospel are drawn into a pastor's plans. Sermons address the "big story," the Christian metanarrative, while not neglecting any "small stories," the micronarrative. Observing where the church is in the Christian year, the preacher becomes a listener to what a particular season is teaching.

Eighth, a Christian habit of being embedded in the ebb and flow of the gospel story shapes believers internally. It seeps into their bones. The months of July to September are ordinary time. The build-up to Christmas is preparation for awe. The months preceding Easter become a period of contemplation, as the meaning of Lent is lived again. Then Easter becomes a rapturous encounter with the risen Christ. Hallelujah! He is risen indeed!

Ninth, the Christian year offers a way to nurture believers of all ages in the patterns of faith. Adults, teens, and children can all be addressed by the story and play, drama and song, sculpture and music. There are endlessly creative ways to tell the Christian story through the course of a year. Let each generation be drawn into the life of God!

Tenth, an alternative pattern of meaning such as is offered by the Christian year yields an alternate set of values that remind us our primary citizenship is not in a political entity, but in the kingdom of heaven. This entails shaping our new identity as members of Christ's body living in the world.

Eleventh, the Christian year can remind us that although we are members of local congregations, we are part of the church catholic, the church universal—"one Lord, one faith, one baptism" (Eph. 4:5).

The joy of knowing, and being reminded, that Christians in other places and communions are joining us as we proceed through the Christian year can energize and unite the body of Christ. There are differences, but our shared unity in Christ should override them all in importance. Christ was born, Christ has died, Christ is risen, and Christ will come again—these are the truths that unite us.

Twelfth, connection to historic, apostolic tradition brings the church's rich past into the present. There are multiple opportunities to introduce today's Christians to the "great cloud of witnesses," to those in the past who have kept the faith, often at the cost of their lives. We need to hear that as Christians we live in the slipstream of salvation history. The Christian wisdom of the ages must be enabled to flow into the present, equipping the church for mission, fulfilling the prayers of our spiritual forebearers.

Practicing the Christian Year

How might the Christian year look in practice in order to form both pastor and people?

First, practice can happen by creating a daily rhythm of prayer, Scripture reading, and listening for God's voice spoken through the events of the year. This includes *gathering* with sisters and brothers for worship and then *sending* them to places of obedient service.

Second, as the theological leader of your congregation, name and preach the content and meaning of God's unfolding story throughout the ebb and flow of the year.

Conclusion

The Christian year has withstood the test of time because it repeats the story of God and his church. Through the centuries, the Christian year has provided a map that leads Christians to relive the Jesus story, helping to form them in faithful obedience in the church, in their families, and in the world. Pastors as stewards have employed the Christian year for forming Christians in "our common salvation

. . . the faith which was once for all delivered to the saints" (Jude v. 3, RSV). Pastors have employed the Christian calendar to teach Christians that in Christ they participate in a new life, a new world, and a new way—a new creation in Christ Jesus their Lord.

Recommended Resources

Gross, Bobby. *Living the Christian Year: Time to Inhabit the Story of God*. Downers Grove, IL: InterVarsity Press, 2009.

LaVigne, Michaele. *Living the Way of Jesus: Practicing the Christian Calendar One Week at a Time*. Kansas City: Foundry, 2019.

Vanderbilt Divinity Library. "FAQ and Related Links." *Revised Common Lectionary*. Accessed March 17, 2022. https://lectionary.library.vanderbilt.edu/faq.php. This website provides excellent resources for planning the Christian year.

Wallace, Robin Knowles. *The Christian Year: A Guide for Worship and Preaching*. Nashville: Abingdon Press, 2011.

Witvliet, John D. "Introduction to the Christian Year." Calvin Institute of Christian Worship. Accessed March 17, 2022. https://worship.calvin.edu/resources/resource-library/introduction-to-the-christian-year-john-witvliet-full-text-/.

11
STEWARD OF ONE'S OWN FAITH DEVELOPMENT

Samuel Carl W. Vassel, DMin

Jesus, Jesus, how I trust Him!

How I've proved Him o'er and o'er!

Jesus, Jesus, precious Jesus!

O for grace to trust Him more![1]

I can still hear my mother and father singing this song with passion in the morning devotions that began every day in my boyhood home. It was their testimony of faith. It witnessed to an established and growing trust in Jesus, enabled by grace and rooted in a proven experience of God's trustworthiness. Both of them were pastors. They were graciously modeling the stewardship of the faith they had received and were passing it on. Through their consistent worship habits, they were planting the faith in me. They were teaching me to "trust Him more."

My more than four decades of pastoral ministry have taught me that what my parents modeled has now become my responsibility to cultivate. This is true of all pastors. What they have received, they must cultivate for themselves before it can be cultivated in others. A pastor is steward of his or her own faith development.

Two Forms of Christian Faith

Two hymns illustrate that Christian faith has two complementary forms: *the faith which is believed* and *the faith which believes*. The hymn "Faith of Our Fathers," written to memorialize martyrs, expresses the first form. "My Faith Looks Up to Thee" expresses the second.

The first verse of "Faith of Our Fathers" is

Faith of our Fathers, living still

In spite of dungeon, fire, and sword!

O how our hearts beat high with joy

Whene'er we hear that glorious word![2]

Here "faith" refers to the Christian faith (Christian identity), including one's faith tradition. The "faith" is a body of beliefs that informs all our thought and life. It is apostolic (e.g., Rom. 6:17; Col. 2:6-7; 2 Thess. 2:15), historic, doctrinal, and confessional. It must be internalized. It shapes our worldview and our ethical structure. The "faith" is primarily objective, for it has a sacrosanct defined content, not to be easily modified. This is what Paul refers to when instructing Titus: "But as for you, teach what befits sound doctrine" (Titus 2:1, RSV).

The second hymn expresses the second form of faith.

> *My Faith looks up to Thee,*
>
> *Thou Lamb of Calvary,*
>
> *Savior Divine!*
>
> *Now hear me while I pray;*
>
> *Take all my guilt away.*
>
> *O let me from this day*
>
> *Be wholly Thine!*[3]

Here "faith" refers to a personal relationship of active trust placed in the "Lamb of Calvary." It expresses one's subjective commitment and experience. It is alive and evidences personal transformation. John Stott explains this kind of faith. "Faith is a reasoning trust, a trust which reckons thoughtfully and confidently upon the trustworthiness of God."[4] So this second form of faith is a relationship with God marked by trust, resulting from compelling evidence. The apostle Paul expressed undiluted trust in God when he addressed his horrified shipmates facing shipwreck on the stormy Mediterranean:

> I urge you to keep up your courage, because not one of you will be lost. . . . Last night an angel of the God to whom I belong and whom I serve stood beside me and said, "Do not be afraid, Paul. You must stand trial before Caesar; and God has graciously given you the lives of all who sail with you." So keep up your courage, men, *for I have faith in God* that it will happen just as he told me. (Acts 27:22-25; emphasis added; cf. Eph. 3:20-21)

When considering the pastor as steward of his or her own faith development, both forms of faith—content and act—must be treasured and cultivated.

The Pastor as Steward

Generally stewardship means guarding and keeping something safe owned by someone else. But stewardship is more than safekeeping. It includes adding value. Think of a hedge fund manager who invests other people's money. He or she must guard what is entrusted and increase its value through prudent investments. As managers, stewards are accountable to investors for safety and increase. This understanding of stewardship is visible in Jesus's parable of the bags of gold (Matt. 25:14-30). The "one talent" recipient thought he had discharged his duty simply by safeguarding what had been entrusted to him. For fear of losing it, he made no effort to add value. Admittedly, security is important. But prioritizing security at the expense of investment earned a stern rebuke from the investor. The steward is called lazy and wicked.

Applying the parable to a pastor's own faith development reveals accountability for the pastor's faith tradition and for the pastor making it relevant, understandable, and accessible in his or her contemporary context. Both things must happen. The faith must be secured, but it must also flourish.

The apostle Paul charged Timothy, "Watch your life and doctrine closely. Persevere in them, because if you do, you will save both yourself and your hearers" (1 Tim. 4:16). Paul also requires Timothy to "guard the good deposit that was entrusted to you—guard it with the help of the Holy Spirit who lives in us" (2 Tim. 1:14; cf. 1 Tim. 2:15). Timothy is expected to exercise stewardship over his life (the content of his character) and doctrine (the content of his teaching). The clear indication is that "who one is" (character) and "what one says" (teaching) directly affect one's ministry to others. Clearly, a pastor is steward of his or her own personal faith development as a prerequisite for cultivating the faith of others. Both responsibilities are essential for serving the mission of God.

The Pastor and Faith Development

Faith development entails growth, maturation, and the flourishing of faith as one's own understanding. This includes an ability to articulate one's theological tradition as well as one's own encounter with the trustworthy God. As is true of other theological traditions, we in the Wesleyan-holiness tradition believe the character of Christ is, by grace, instilled and cultivated by the Holy Spirit. For us this is the gold standard and observable outcome of faith development. On the one hand, this entails an ever-increasing understanding of what "looking like Christ"—Christlikeness—means. On the other hand, faith entails holistic transformation and formation under the Holy Spirit's guidance.

In our theological tradition the structure of our faith is famously called the Wesleyan quadrilateral: Scripture, tradition, reason, and experience.[5] Scripture is regarded as trustworthy and authoritative. It forms the foundation for the other parts of the quadrilateral. Scripture is reflected upon through the lenses of tradition, reason, and experience. This entails perceiving more and more clearly the Christian faith and embodying that faith in a holy life. It also entails an increasing ability to articulately bear witness to the Christian faith for the church and in the world.

A pastor must therefore be exemplary with reference to the more cognitive dimensions of the faith and also in Christlike character. While faith development in both forms occurs by grace alone, one must consciously cooperate with the Holy Spirit. The flourishing of faith is not something about which one can be passive. One must be a good steward of the process. Let's consider this dimension of our stewardship.

Stewarding One's Own Faith Development

I understood my pastoral role as focused on five main areas: (1) preaching and teaching, (2) leading the church in worship, (3) rightly administering the sacraments, (4) administering the affairs of the church, and (5) pastoral care. Given these responsibilities, spiritual burnout is inevitable unless I have a developing faith from which I minister to others. I have noticed that inherent in the pastoral task are opportunities for faith development as one ministers in the five mentioned areas. I have experienced all five as *means of grace.*[6]

Preaching and teaching has been a main source of faith development. The saying "The sermon comes to the preacher first" has been true for me. True to what Paul said about Scripture, I have been taught, rebuked, corrected, and trained in righteousness through sermon preparation and proclamation (2 Tim. 3:16-17). I have regularly identified the message as speaking first to me while I grapple with the existential questions of my congregation, my community, and my sociopolitical context. I routinely apply the Wesleyan quadrilateral to those questions. In the process, God speaks to me about himself, my congregation, and my world.[7] Inevitably my faith, as the Christian faith and as my relationship of reasoning trust in God, is challenged, stretched, and strengthened.

An example of faith development in both dimensions has been the significance of human dignity in light of a history of systemic racial injustice experienced by people of color in the United States. This is an existential question facing black, brown, and Asian people in the congregations and communities where I preach and teach. An intensified emphasis has been placed on the Christian belief that everyone is created in God's image (Gen. 9:6; Act 17:27-29). More particularly, I consider the atoning death of Jesus Christ applicable to demolishing racial discrimination, which is essential to reconcile "one new humanity" to God (Eph. 2:15-16). I cannot now think of the atoning work of Christ without seeing this as being at the heart of the salvific preaching and teaching I am privileged to practice. The Christ I am called to represent, who lovingly gave himself to remove the separation between God and humans, and between humans, invites me in obedience to the Holy Spirit to represent the Redeemer in the church and the world. To repeat, preaching and teaching requires that I grow in my ability to hear and address the existential questions of my congregation and to "add" to my faith in the process.

Faith development is inseparable from the Holy Spirit enabling a pastor to love the Lord with all his or her heart, soul, and mind (Matt. 22:37). Loving the Lord with one's entire mind requires disciplined study. This includes reading widely not only in biblical studies and theology but also in informative fields beyond. This helps ensure that what a pastor proclaims can be heard in a contemporary context. As one's faith develops as a heartwarming relationship of trust in God, its reflective theological content must also increase. Then one can minister both passionately and thoughtfully.

Aligning the Two Dimensions of Faith

A pastor represents the faith tradition of the congregation he or she leads. However, being faithful to one's theological tradition can make a pastor a prisoner of tradition. That need not happen if one's faith tradition expresses and is with conviction enlivened by a pulsating faith.

Church historian Jaroslav Pelikan (1923–2006) distinguished between traditionalism and tradition. "Tradition," he said, "is the living faith of the dead; traditionalism is the dead faith of the living."[8] Accepting and preserving one's faith tradition is insufficient. It must be made understandable as a living faith that answers contemporary existential questions. Otherwise, tradition becomes impotent, to be pronounced "dead" while in the custody of a pastor whose responsibility was to make of it a living faith.

Stewardship of a pastor's own faith development requires a creative restatement of his or her faith tradition for a congregation. Its essential character is maintained while making its intended meaning live in a way that actually connects with recipients. "Tradition," Pelikan added, "lives in conversation with the past, while remembering where we are and when we are and that it is we who have to decide."[9]

Diane Leclerc draws upon Gregory Clapper and Theodore Runyon to explain the positive faith value of tradition for John Wesley. While for Wesley, Christianity involved right doctrine (orthodoxy) and right action (orthopraxy), something in his vision of faith goes much deeper. "Ortho*kardia*—the right heart" must be added.[10] Without this there is no Christian faith. Runyon suggested the term "orthopathy" to express the vital relationship. Wesley said true religion is never a matter of intellectual assent alone. With the heart one believes.[11]

Developing Faith as Reasoning Trust

We have defined "faith" above as "reasoning trust" in God. It must be emphasized that the revelation of God to us is always at God's initiative. Its fulfillment however relies upon an openness to receive it (John 1:9-13). Jesus said, "Whoever has ears, let them hear" (Matt. 11:15; Mark 4:23; Luke 8:8; cf. Rev. 2:7, 11, 17, 29; 3:6, 13, 22). A pastor receives the illumining promptings of the Holy Spirit that yields a relationship, a life of reasoning trust in our trustworthy God.

For me these graced encounters have involved a comprehensive paradigm shift. As pastors we must habitually engage in practices that cultivate "reasoning trust" that expands our knowledge of God's character and ways, of his being trustworthy. The Old Testament celebrates God's trustworthiness and calls it *hesed*, God's steadfast love or mercy (e.g., Exod. 34:6; 1 Chron. 16:34; Job 10:12; Pss. 106:1; 130:7). The more one knows God's holy love revealed in Jesus Christ, the more one intensifies his or her conviction that God is trustworthy, and the richer one's faith becomes. The apostle Paul exclaimed, "Oh, the depth of the riches of the wisdom and knowledge of God! How unsearchable his judgments, and his paths beyond tracing out!" (Rom. 11:33). He told the Philippians, "I want to know Christ—yes, to know the power of his resurrection and participation in his sufferings, becoming like him in his death, and so, somehow, attaining to the resurrection from the dead" (Phil. 3:10-11).

There are historic practices, spiritual disciplines, or means of grace used by the Spirit to cultivate the kind of doxological trust Paul expressed. Call them "attitudes of the heart expressed as worship." They include worship, singing (corporate and private), Scripture study, meditative reading, prayer, "blessed subtraction" (fasting), receiving the Eucharist, serving those in need, and small group fellowship. Increasing love for God and sacrificial love for others are the result. Call this progressive sanctification, increasing in Christlikeness (2 Cor. 3:18).

Marriage: A Case in Point

For those who are married, an absolutely vital focus of a pastor's faith development is his or her marriage. Paul urges the Ephesian Christians to be "filled with the Spirit" (Eph. 5:18). Then he shows what being filled with the Spirit looks like (vv. 21-33) by citing marriage as a principal illustration. Mutual loving submission to one another is the centerpiece of Christlikeness in Spirit-filled marriages (cf. Phil. 2:1-11). Paul intensifies the importance and character of marriage as an example of being filled with the Spirit; he says marriage correctly understood is a key for unlocking the mystery of Christ's relationship with the church (Eph. 5:32-33).

Christian Conferencing

I have been the grateful beneficiary of all the Christian disciplines. By far the most important has been the grace derived from small group fellowship. In Wesleyan terminology this is referred to as "Christian conferencing." I have been a part of a small group of pastors for twenty-eight years. In that fellowship, I have experienced what Jesus promised in Matthew 18:20: "For where two or three gather in my name, there am I with them." I have experienced unconditional acceptance, loving support, mutual respect, honest accountability, and, above all, the trustworthy presence of God. If I were to advise my fellow clergy, it would be that stewardship of one's faith development must never occur in isolation from other Christian ministers. Find grace for the journey in the communal fellowship, encouragement, and accountability gained through Christian conference. Your faith will strengthen because in that setting you will encounter a trustworthy God.

> *'Tis so sweet to trust in Jesus,*
> *Just to take Him at His Word,*
> *Just to rest upon His promise,*
> *Just to know: "Thus saith the Lord."*[12]

Recommended Resources

Leclerc, Diane. *Discovering Christian Holiness: The Heart of Wesleyan-Holiness Theology*. Kansas City: Beacon Hill Press of Kansas City, 2010.

Noble, T. A. *Holy Trinity: Holy People: The Historic Doctrine of Christian Perfecting*. Eugene, OR: Cascade Books, 2013.

Tracy, Wesley D., E. Dee Freeborn, Janine Tartaglia, and Morris A. Weigelt. *The Upward Call: Spiritual Formation and the Holy Life*. Kansas City: Beacon Hill Press of Kansas City, 1994.

Willard, Dallas, Bill Thrall, Bruce McNicol, Keith J. Matthews, Bill Hull, Keith Meyer, Peggy Reynoso et al. *The Kingdom Life: A Practical Theology of Discipleship and Spiritual Formation*. Colorado Springs: NavPress, 2010.

Wright, N. T. *After You Believe: Why Christian Character Matters*. New York: HarperCollins, 2010.

12
STEWARD OF THE MISSION OF GOD

Dean Flemming, PhD

I USED TO BE a "rock star." Well, not *literally*. But I did serve for nearly a quarter century as a missionary with the Church of the Nazarene. And when I visited local churches during my home assignment, people often treated me something like a cross between David Livingstone and Mother Teresa! I constantly felt the urge to upgrade my "walking on water" technique! Missionaries—and, for that matter, *missions* in general—were considered a bit exotic, exceptional, and extraordinary. In the popular Christian imagination, *mission* was something that especially heroic, God-called individuals did somewhere else in the world. Everyone else prayed for, gave to, and admired that unique calling.

But is *mission* simply about outreach activities, especially those that happen in another culture?[1] Or is the whole notion of mission much bigger than that? In this chapter, we'll start by asking precisely that question: What is mission, and what is God's role in it? Then we'll explore the key part that local church pastors play in stewarding the mission of God. That involves both leading congregations into a richer understanding of mission and energizing them to get caught up in God's mission in who they are, what they do, and what they say. Finally, we'll consider what it means for local congregations to engage in mission within the public spaces of their world.

What Is Mission?

During much of the time I served as a parish minister and a global missionary, people in my ecclesial tribe generally agreed on what mission, or *missions*, was about. It had to do with things such as

- sending missionaries to serve in far-off places,
- yearly Faith Promise conventions,
- potluck dinners when a missionary came to speak,
- annual mission trips,
- line items on a church budget,
- praying for cross-cultural missionaries and ministries,
- soup kitchens and food pantries, and

- efforts to evangelize unbelievers and multiply churches throughout the world.

Don't get me wrong. These are all *good* things (including the pot-luck dinners!). But they represent only *part* of what mission is about, not all of it. You'll notice that these items are primarily *activities*, things we *do*. But mission, first and foremost, concerns who we *are*. It is anchored in our participation in the life of God, not simply what we do *for* God. We often talk about the *church's* mission in the world. But that can sound like mission is mainly about *us* and what *we* do.

Mission, above all, is about *God*. And when we start thinking about the mission of *God*, the *missio Dei*, the whole notion of mission suddenly expands. Enormously! Mission has to do with all that God is up to in the world. It's about "God's massive purpose to bring wholeness and redemption to the entire creation, especially people from every nation, as well as what we as God's people are called to be, do, and say as we participate in God's great purpose."[2] Looking at mission from this perspective can't help but stretch our imaginations, like a balloon being filled with air. It guards us against thinking about mission mainly in terms of outreach programs, strategies, or numbers. It poses an audacious question: Are we, the church, caught up in God's sweeping purpose for the world to make *"everything* new" (Rev. 21:5; emphasis added)? If we are, then aligning ourselves with God's missional purposes surely includes the following:

- Not only bringing people to faith but also forming communities of mature, Christlike disciples (Eph. 4:12-16; Col. 1:27-28)
- Actively caring for the creation that God loves, delights in, and wants to restore (Ps. 145:9; Rom. 8:19-23; Col. 1:20)
- Resisting racism and systems that peddle injustice, by our words, our attitudes, and our actions (Ps. 103:6; Luke 4:18-19)
- Caring for the poor, the homeless, the trafficked, the immigrant, and the marginalized (Deut. 10:12-19; Matt. 25:31-46)
- Publicly announcing through our gathered and scattered *worship* that God alone sits on the throne of the universe and that

the idols and ideologies of our cultures do not (Phil. 2:10-11; Rev. 4–5)

- Not only speaking the gospel but *becoming* the gospel, as we live out the pattern of Jesus's self-giving love both *before* a watching world and *within* the public spaces of our world (Phil. 2:5-8; 1 Pet. 2:21-23)

And that's just a start.

For local congregations, then, mission involves more than sending and supporting cross-cultural missionaries, although that's a vital part of it. A sound biblical theology of mission calls the whole people of God to get caught up in the whole mission of God, both locally and globally, at every level of human need. It reminds us that *mission* isn't simply one part of what the church *does*; it's what the church *is*. The mission is God's, but the church is God's chosen instrument for fulfilling his restoring, life-giving purposes in the world. The church, in its very DNA, is missional. Christopher Wright points out that the notion of a "missional church" has gotten a lot of buzz in recent years. However, from a theological perspective, the church has *always* been missional. In fact, the term "missional church" is about as redundant as a "young infant." If a church isn't missional, it isn't the church.[3]

What does this wide and wonderful understanding of mission mean for pastors and leaders of local congregations? How do we *steward* the mission of God?

Equipping for Mission

I will rely on the apostle Paul as a dialogue partner in exploring what it means for pastors to steward God's mission. Paul didn't function as a local church pastor in the modern sense. But he did carry a profound sense of pastoral responsibility toward the churches he founded. His pastoral concern included his desire to shape young believers into mature, missional communities of Christ followers. That's part of why Paul wrote letters to local congregations—to energize and equip them to participate in God's great purposes in the world where they live.

Despite his unique apostolic calling, Paul couldn't have imagined a "lone ranger" ministry. Writing to the Philippians, he celebrates their "partnership in the gospel" from the beginning until the present (Phil. 1:5). In the context, this language spotlights that they partnered *with* Paul in the ministry of the good news. What did that gospel partnership entail? If we track the missional footprints in Philippians, they include these features:[4]

- Practical support of Paul's ministry, both through financial generosity (Phil. 4:15-16) and sending coworkers to minister to Paul (2:25-30)
- Intercessory prayer for Paul (1:19)
- Suffering along with Paul for the sake of the gospel (1:30; 4:14)
- Living out their public lives in a way that's worthy of the gospel (1:27)
- Bearing witness to the gospel in Philippi (1:27, 28; 2:15-16)
- Adopting Jesus's example of self-giving love, both inside and outside the church (2:5-8)

Paul both affirms these Christians for sharing in God's mission and seeks to strengthen and shape that missional partnership in this letter.

Shouldn't local church pastors and leaders fulfill a similar role on behalf of the congregations they serve? Following Paul's lead, stewarding the mission of God in local congregations involves at least four dimensions: knowing, being, doing, and telling.

Making Sure We're on Mission

Paul made certain that his converts knew what they were part of. He painted his vision of God's mission on a cosmic canvas:

- "[God] has made known to us the mystery of his will, according to his good pleasure that he set forth in Christ, as a plan for the fullness of time, to gather up all things in him, things in heaven and things on earth" (Eph. 1:9-10, NRSV).

- "Through [Christ] God was pleased to reconcile to himself all things, whether on earth or in heaven, by making peace through the blood of his cross" (Col. 1:20, NRSV).
- "For [Christ] is our peace; in his flesh he has made both groups into one and has broken down the dividing wall, that is, the hostility between us" (Eph. 2:14; cf. vv. 15-16).

For Paul, the gospel was about far more than getting individuals saved so that they could reserve a place in heaven. It was about God's healing, reconciling, peacemaking purposes in the world, in and through the crucified and risen Christ, in every arena of life.

This carries implications for pastoral ministry. Part of our ministry of preaching, teaching, and discipling must involve expanding our local congregation's grasp of what God is up to in the world and how we are called to join him in that purpose. For example, does God's mission involve overturning divisions based on race, ethnicity, nationality, or economic status? Paul certainly thinks so. He invites us into a "new humanity" in which the dividing walls crumble (Eph. 2:14-15, NRSV), where "there is no longer Greek and Jew, circumcised and uncircumcised, barbarian, Scythian, slave and free," but where "Christ is all and in all" (Col. 3:11, NRSV). Too often congregations are shaped more by their social experience than they are by the biblical vision of new creation in Christ. Our discipling ministry must surely include helping congregants *and ourselves*, as leaders, recognize our blind spots—how we might participate in systems that promote racial hierarchies and inequities, treat deep-seated nationalism as if it were a *Christian* virtue, or succumb to ethnocentrism ("Our way is better!") and suspicion of foreigners.

But it's not enough simply to teach congregations the implications of the mission of God. We must also lead them into practices that embody that understanding. Can we, for example, find ways to reverse the power inequalities in our churches and intentionally give voice to marginalized and ignored people in decision-making structures, financial priorities, or outreach planning? Are there opportunities to enter sustained partnerships of conversation and service with congregations from a different racial, cultural, or social demographic than our own? This is risky stuff. It may spark misinterpretation and pushback. But it's part of what it means to participate in what God is doing in the world.

Embodying the Gospel

For Paul, it's not enough simply to *proclaim* the gospel. God's people must *become* the gospel in who they are and how they live.[5] That begins with the apostle himself. In a context where street preachers often peddled their teaching to make money, Paul assures a local congregation, "We were delighted to share with you not only the gospel of God but *our lives* as well" (1 Thess. 2:8; emphasis added). Paul knows well that if *he* is discredited, then so is the mission he fulfills and the gospel he declares. Instead of falsifying God's word, Paul testifies, "*We commend ourselves* to the conscience of everyone in the sight of God" (2 Cor. 4:2, NRSV; emphasis added). He *re*-presents the gospel of Christ's self-giving love in blood and bone.

If ever it were crucial for pastors to embody the gospel, now is the time. Our hearts break over each new revelation of a Christian leader besmirching his or her message and mission with "un-gospel-like" attitudes and actions. Such conduct feeds the cynicism of the watching world toward the church. Our humble, self-giving behavior toward others, our integrity in finances and sexual conduct, our commitment to "[speak] the truth in love" (Eph. 4:15) in social-media posts—all model our message for those both inside and outside the church. A gospel that isn't embodied isn't credible.

At the same time, "becoming the gospel" extends to the churches we serve. For Paul, mission isn't simply what the church *does*, but what the church *is*. The church is a living temple (1 Cor. 3:16-17; 2 Cor. 6:16; Eph. 2:21) filled with the presence of God and making God's glory visible in the world. Our God-given identity as God's people means not only embracing but embodying the gospel in our holiness, our unity, and our cross-shaped love (Phil. 2:1-8, 14-15). The same "mindset" that led Jesus on the downward path to "death on a cross" must govern both our gathered life in community and our scattered witness in the world (vv. 5-11).[6]

No less than for the apostle himself, the church's mission is inextricably tied to its Christlike character. On the positive side, God's people should abound in love, not only for other Christians but also for all—that is, outsiders (1 Thess. 3:12; cf. Phil. 4:5; 1 Thess. 5:15). If Christians live blameless lives within a corrupt culture, they will carry a light-bearing witness to those around them (Phil. 2:15). Holiness is missional. For example, Christian families can model fidelity and sacrificial love in spaces where abuse, conflict, and throwaway relationships are too often the cultural template. On the flip side, when we grumble and argue among ourselves, when we're torn apart over political loyalties, we risk sabotaging our reconciling mission in the world (v. 14). Too often, the way God's people treat one another, especially on social media, projects anything *but* good news to a watching world.

Practicing the Gospel

Pastors can steward the mission of God in their congregations by encouraging not only missional *identity* but also missional *practice*.[7] For Paul and his churches, "doing" the gospel took various forms. In Philippians, it included caring for Paul's financial and material needs through their gifts and the help of their representative Epaphroditus (4:10-20). Local congregations also supported his mission by sending him on his way (1 Cor. 16:6; 2 Cor. 1:16; Rom. 15:24), providing practical assistance for his missionary work. In the ministry of generosity to others, Paul led by example. It's striking that Paul pressed the pause button on his plans for an evangelistic mission to Spain so that he could first deliver a "compassionate ministries" offering from the Gentile churches to suffering Jewish Christians in Jerusalem (Rom. 15:23-25). Today, as well, local congregations are unlikely to embrace a pattern of missional generosity unless leaders model that priority before them.

Paul encouraged ordinary Christians to partner with him in God's mission in other ways, including intercessory prayer (e.g., Rom. 15:30-32; Eph. 6:19; Col. 4:3-4), mutual encouragement (Rom. 1:11-12), and suffering along with Paul for the gospel's sake (2 Cor. 1:6-7; Phil. 1:30; 4:14). Even congregational worship can provide an occasion for bearing witness to outsiders. Paul urges the Corinthians to practice restraint in exercising their spiritual gifts, in part, so that visiting unbelievers might hear God's words clearly and, as a result, bow down and worship God (1 Cor. 14:23-25).

Paul never encourages God's people to cut off connections with non-Christians (5:9-10). Rather, congregations must engage their world in transforming ways. In Philippians, Paul tells church members to dwell on virtues that were widely recognized and valued in Greco-Roman culture (4:8). Instead of rejecting these values as worldly, he affirms them as points of contact with his world, as long as they are consistent with the self-giving example of Christ (v. 9).

It's clear that Paul sees no single cookie-cutter pattern for local congregations to engage in God's mission. Likewise, *our* mission practice requires creativity, flexibility, and multiple avenues for touching the lives of people, both locally and throughout the world.

Narrating the Gospel

What about telling the good news to others and leading them to mature faith in Christ? How do we steward that dimension of mission? Obviously, it starts with our own passion for the gospel. Paul pictures himself as a "[steward] of God's mysteries" (1 Cor. 4:1, NRSV) and a "servant of [the] gospel" (Col. 1:23, NRSV), accountable to God alone for faithful service (1 Cor. 4:2). That stewardship involves not only announcing the good news to others "so that they may be saved" (1 Thess. 2:16, NRSV; cf. Rom. 1:16; 1 Cor. 9:19-23) but also proclaiming and teaching the gospel to believers in order to "present everyone mature in Christ" (Col. 1:28, NRSV; cf. 1 Thess. 2:12).

Does that ministry of speaking the gospel extend to congregations as a whole? We might be surprised that Paul never directly urges his churches to join him in proclaiming the gospel to unbelievers or prays that they might do so. But there's more to the story. Local congregations may not preach publicly like their apostle, yet Paul assumes they would speak the good news to outsiders in the course of their ordinary lives. Paul advises the Colossians, "Let your speech always be gracious, seasoned with salt, so that you may know how you ought to answer everyone" (Col. 4:6, NRSV). Here Paul imagines Christians, not so much initiating an intentional evangelistic strategy as responding to outsiders' questions or objections during their daily interactions.

Philippians gives particular attention to Christians telling the gospel. In Philippians 1, Paul spotlights the courageous witness of the Roman believers as an example for the Philippians to follow (v. 14). Later, he pictures the whole church shining like lights in a dark world, "holding out the word of life" (2:16, author's translation).[8] It seems clear that Paul wants church members to tell the good-news story in ways that are appropriate to their everyday lives and relationships. Speaking the gospel is married to living the gospel in every dimension of life (Col. 4:5-6).

In recent decades, telling the gospel has faded in importance in some Christian circles. My students sometimes quote the saying attributed to Francis of Assisi, "Preach the gospel at all times, *and if necessary*, use words," with the implication that words may *not* be necessary. A pastor friend once told me that he bore witness in his neighborhood by practicing love and compassion: doing odd jobs, raking leaves for seniors, or listening to people's family and job concerns. "But I don't talk about my faith. People don't trust words. I let my *life* communicate the gospel." Yes, but . . . at some point people need to hear the transforming story that gives reason for our loving actions. After all, it is good *news*! And pastors must provide ways of equipping congregations to do that more confidently and faithfully in their world.

Finally, Paul implores congregations to support his missionary proclamation with prayer: "Pray . . . for me, that whenever I speak, words may be given me so that I will fearlessly make known the mystery of the gospel" (Eph. 6:19; cf. Col. 4:3-4). Part of our stewardship of the gospel involves encouraging churches to pray for those whom God has called to specific evangelistic ministries, whether locally or in mission settings throughout the world.

Mobilizing the Local Church for Mission

H. Al Gilbert asks, "What could happen if everyone in your church viewed life through the mission of God? What if the *whole church* 'got it': every heart on fire, every skill and gift deployed, every relationship and circumstance submitted to the lordship of Christ, the people of God understanding and living out the mission of God?"[9] Too idealistic? Perhaps. But somehow we need to help move local congregations from a *missions* mentality, where the mission of God is only about sending God-called cross-cultural workers across a body of salt water, to a *missional* mentality, which sees mission as a lifestyle for every follower of Jesus.

Now I believe in cross-cultural missions! I served as that kind of missionary for nearly a quarter of a century. And I am convinced that local church pastors are the essential link for congregations to passionately engage in the task of discipling the nations. If a pastor doesn't carry a vision for global mission, neither will the church. If pastors don't challenge young people and adults to be open to God's calling to global mission, or lead the church in praying that might happen (Matt. 9:38), it's unlikely that many in their congregations will hear and respond to God's call.

But stewarding the mission of God also compels us to help congregations live out the mission of being, doing, and telling the gospel on their everyday turf. Gregg Okesson advocates a "public missiology," which invites congregations to engage in public witness by word and life in the complex spaces where they live, work, rest, play, and relate to each other.[10] Church buildings can function as community-oriented spaces, where "the lines between the church and community are crossed and re-crossed many times a day."[11] Church members are "sent" into their public worlds of health needs, creation care, social inequities, kids' sports leagues, and book clubs, bearing witness to a gospel that is robust enough to seek not only personal salvation but also transformation of all the arenas of public life. This reminds me of what Paul says to the congregation in Philippi: literally, "live out your *citizenship* [your public, corporate life] in a manner worthy of the gospel of Christ" (Phil. 1:27, author's translation). As we live out our lives in the public square, we must visibly embody the good news about Christ.

What does that look like in practice? Here's an example. One of my former students, Philip, and his brother Cris lead the ministry of Church in Action (*Kirche in Aktion*) in the Rhine-Main region of Germany.[12] Compelled by a vision of heaven breaking into the public spaces of their world, these young leaders have invited Christians into a robust, many-sided mission in and for their cities. That ministry includes worship gatherings in public places such as cafés, pubs, theaters, homes for seniors, and restaurants, as well as discipling small group "communities on mission." But they also serve the marginalized around them, offering housing to refugee families and mobile game stations for their children, holding youth clubs for urban teenagers, providing sex workers friendship and help filling out insurance forms, delivering food to the homeless, engaging seniors in coffee-hour conversations, and organizing international ministry trips. Through word and deed, they are living out the transforming gospel in their public world.

Closer to home, my niece and two nephews all work in the arts, writing and recording music and producing TV shows. They are not

"Christian artists" as such, but they embody the way of Christ in a public arena that sorely needs the touch of God's grace.

Mission as a lifestyle won't look the same from church to church. As pastors, we can help church members identify their gifts, passions, and interpersonal networks, as well as the public spaces they move in and out of. At the same time, we can help Christians understand the identity and context of their congregations. What, for example, is the social fabric of the area surrounding the church? Who lives there and what are the significant needs? And what specific global ministries and partnerships is the congregation gifted and positioned to engage in? Pastors as stewards enable missional congregations to intersect their gifts and passions with the world's great needs.

Measuring Our Mission

How do we know if we're "on mission"? How do we measure our "success" in the stewardship God has entrusted to us? Although the glory of the twentieth-century church growth movement has faded significantly, pastors and district leaders still often feel pressure to "produce" in terms of numbers and programs. Paul's goal was not simply to win converts but to shape and nurture congregations of young believers into mature Christian communities that are conformed to the likeness of Christ (Phil. 2:5). If the global COVID-19 pandemic has taught us anything, it is that we can't measure the effectiveness of our ministry solely or even primarily by the number of people in a sanctuary on a Sunday morning.

Depth is missional. Mission flows out of who we *are*. Only if we *become* the people we're called to be can we offer a credible witness of word and life that is attractive to a watching world. Reflecting on the remarkable expansion of the church in the first few centuries, historian Alan Kreider asks, "How . . . did the church grow? . . . The most reliable means of communicating the attractiveness of the faith to others and enticing them to investigate things further was the Christians' character, bearing, and behavior."[13] Is it so different today?

Conclusion

Pastors are gifted with the stunning privilege of equipping and energizing God's people to get caught up in the *missio Dei*. That begins by helping congregations grasp the beauty and breadth of God's purposes in the world. It includes mobilizing believers to cast their vision beyond their local scene, to become *world* Christians, to engage in the adventure of making disciples of *all nations*, whether by praying, giving, educating, partnering, sending, or going. But local church pastors must also inspire a seamless understanding of mission, which embraces *both* the local and the global. They must lead congregations to *become* the missional people God has called them to be, to discover how to put God's restoring mission into *practice* in ways that connect with the specific needs of their community, and to *speak* the good news as God gives opportunity within the everyday spaces of their public world. Finally, there's the power of example. We can *steward* God's mission by *living* God's mission. May we be found faithful to that calling and privilege (1 Cor. 4:1-2).

Recommended Resources

Flemming, Dean. *Foretaste of the Future: Reading Revelation in Light of God's Mission.* Downers Grove, IL: IVP Academic, forthcoming.

———. *Recovering the Full Mission of God: A Biblical Perspective on Being, Doing and Telling.* Downers Grove, IL: IVP Academic, 2013.

———. *Why Mission?* Nashville: Abingdon Press, 2015.

Gorman, Michael J. *Becoming the Gospel: Paul, Participation, and Mission.* Grand Rapids: Eerdmans, 2015.

Okesson, Gregg. *A Public Missiology: How Local Churches Witness to a Complex World.* Grand Rapids: Baker Academic, 2020.

Wright, Christopher J. H. *The Mission of God's People: A Biblical Theology of the Church's Mission.* Grand Rapids: Zondervan, 2010.

———. *The Mission of God: Unlocking the Bible's Grand Narrative.* Downers Grove, IL: IVP Academic, 2006.

Appendix for Chapter 3,
"Steward of the Scriptures"
THE FIVE Ws
C. Jeanne Serrão, PhD

HERE IS A SERIES of questions and answers that can be used as a guide for adult Bible study or for teaching.

I. *Who?* This question reminds us that we need to identify both the author and the reader. In narrative sections, the speaker and listener also need to be identified. First, try to answer the question from your own reading and, second, from commentaries: Who are the authors and/or speakers and the readers and/or listeners, and how may they be described?

A. The point of view of the speaker and/or author:

1. Read the chosen text and identify who is speaking. It may be a narrator, so there is only one author. There may be one or several people speaking. If so, describe each one. Often we can find clues about the author in the first few verses of a book. Rarely are there clear descriptions of the speakers or the author. Look between the lines for clues. Consult commentary introductions.

2. We can learn more about the speaker and author by looking at their choice of and arrangement of words, treatment of the subject matter, use of evidence, and how they argue for their position. Study the use of emotion to see how the speaker or author tries to persuade his or her audience.

B. The point of view of the listener and/or reader:
Here we focus on the audience. The type of audience affects the arguments, tone of voice, and the speaker's word choices. Different audiences can account for differences in style a speaker or author uses. Look for clues in the text that indicate the kind of audience the speaker (or author) is addressing.

C. Cultural considerations:
Sometimes the text and our own understanding of how things work are not enough. This is why we go to books

that tell us what has been discovered about the general customs, authority structures, relationships (marriage, friendship, employment), and commerce (agricultural and urban) in the first-century world. The combination of cultural considerations with actual descriptions in the text will give us a clearer picture of everyday life and the people we are trying to understand.

II. *When?* Here we are not so much seeking a date as we are concerned with the historical setting. What events come before and after the passage or story under consideration?

   A. Look for clues in the chapters prior to and after your passage for the historical context. Does it mention a political or civil event? Do you see names of rulers or officials? Try to answer the question, How does this historical setting affect how the people would have heard or read the passage?

   B. In commentaries, read the introductory sections to the book of the Bible being studied. Introductory textbooks for the Old or New Testament will also help. Learn if the author or the audience would have been familiar with the history of your passage. From their historical perspective, how would they have understood the message?

III. *Where?* What is the geographical setting of the text being studied? What does it contribute to its meaning?

   A. Look for clues in passages prior to and after your text that indicate geographical setting. Is a town, mountain, body of water, or city named? Are animals or crops spoken of? Try to answer the question, Does the geographical setting affect how people would have originally heard or read your text?

   B. In commentary introductory sections to the book being studied, learn whether the author or the audience would have been familiar with the geography of your passage. How would they have understood the text from their geographical perspective?

IV. *What?* What does the passage say to the original audience?

   A. What is the content of the letter? (Construct your own broad outline of the complete letter.)

   B. What is the literary context of your passage? (What comes before it? What comes after it?)

   C. What is the form or genre of your passage? What is its rhetorical function? (What kind of literature is this—poetry, narrative, or some other genre? What is the literature used for?)

   D. What is the subject and purpose of your passage? (Identify the main clauses and subordinate clauses so you can grasp the main purpose of the passage.)

   E. What is the best wording of your text? (According to your commentaries, what manuscript problems and/or differences exist in the Greek text?)

   F. What discrepancies exist between English translations? Why? (Compare at least the NIV, KJV, NRSV, and NASB.)

   G. What is the content of your passage? (Outline your passage in detail.)

   H. Commentary: This is the main part of the exegesis. Comment on your passage, clause by clause (or main point by main point), pointing out the grammatical structure and the meaning of each clause. (Do research on key words in your passage, and include the information in your commentary.)

V. *Why?* The *why* question has three parts: (1) Why did the speaker say what he or she said? (2) Why did the author include this section in his or her book? (3) Why is the text important for us today? Step back mentally from the *who, what*, *when*, and *where* questions and answers, and think about what you have learned in the process. What is the central point of the passage? Why is it important to each of the following: the initial story (i.e., a narrative with a speaker different from the book's author), the author who is writing the book, and today? This is creative thinking time!

NOTES

Introduction

    1. Chantal Delsol, *Icarus Fallen*, trans. Robin Dick (Wilmington, DE: ISI Books, 2003), 28-29.

    2. Randy L. Maddox, "Reflections on Responsible Grace," *Wesleyan Theological Journal* 56, no. 1 (Spring 2021): 131.

    3. Randy L. Maddox, *Responsible Grace: John Wesley's Practical Theology* (Nashville: Kingswood Books, 1994), 16.

Chapter 1

    1. Eugene H. Peterson, *The Jesus Way: A Conversation on the Ways That Jesus Is the Way* (Grand Rapids: Eerdmans, 2007), 31.

    2. N. T. Wright, *Simply Good News: Why the Gospel Is News and What Makes It Good* (New York: HarperOne, 2015), 4.

    3. Tim Keller, "Tim Keller," in "Gospel Definitions," comp. Trevin Wax, The Gospel Coalition, updated September 2012, https://media.thegospelcoalition.org/static-blogs/trevin-wax/files/2009/09/Gospel-Definitions.pdf.

    4. Andy Crouch, *Culture Making: Recovering Our Creative Calling* (Downers Grove, IL: InterVarsity Press, 2013), 146.

    5. Scot McKnight, "Kingdom Gospel 7," *Jesus Creed* (blog), Beliefnet.com, accessed June 18, 2021, https://www.beliefnet.com/columnists/jesuscreed/2009/05/kingdom-gospel-7.html.

    6. John Piper and N. T. Wright, "The Justification Debate: A Primer," *Christianity Today*, June 26, 2009, 35.

    7. *The Book of Common Prayer* (New York: Seabury Press, 1979), 363.

Chapter 2

    1. Eugene H. Peterson, *Working the Angles: The Shape of Pastoral Integrity* (Grand Rapids: Eerdmans, 1987), 2.

    2. "The Lord's Supper," *Manual, Church of the Nazarene, 2017–2021*, para. 13 (Kansas City: Nazarene Publishing House, 2017), 35.

    3. Ronald Rolheiser, *The Holy Longing: The Search for a Christian Spirituality* (New York: Doubleday, 1999), 79.

    4. Ibid.

    5. Sam Powell, *The Trinity* (Kansas City: Foundry, 2020), 65.

    6. Brueggemann speaks of this in an interview on YouTube: "Preaching Moment 012: Walter Brueggemann," YouTube video, 2:39, posted by "Working Preacher," September 23, 2008, https://www.youtube.com/watch?v=J5nPlPMDDQ0.

7. The language of the *Manual, Church of the Nazarene, 2017–2021*, paras. 515-516.15.

8. William H. Willimon, *Pastor: The Theology and Practice of Ordained Ministry* (Nashville: Abingdon, 2002), 60.

9. Attributed to Teresa of Avila, quoted in Rolheiser, *Holy Longing*, 73.

10. *Manual, Church of the Nazarene, 2017–2021*, para. 11, p. 33.

11. Ibid.

12. Emil Brunner, *The Word and the World* (London: Student Christian Movement Press, 1931), 108.

13. *Manual, Church of the Nazarene, 2017–2021*, para. 11, p. 33.

Chapter 3

1. Kenneth Berding, "The Crisis of Biblical Illiteracy," *Biola Magazine*, May 29, 2014, https://www.biola.edu/blogs/biola-magazine/2014/the-crisis-of-biblical-illiteracy.

2. Bruce J. Malina, *The New Testament World*, 3rd ed. (Louisville, KY: Westminster John Knox Press, 2001), 81-107.

3. Lenny Luchetti, "Narrative Preaching," Wesley Seminary at Indiana Wesleyan University, August 23, 2010, https://wesleyanseminary.wordpress.com/2010/08/23/narrative-preaching-by-lenny-luchetti/.

4. "Simchat Torah," Hebcal, accessed March 19, 2022, https://www.hebcal.com/holidays/simchat-torah-2021.

Chapter 4

1. Wolfhart Pannenberg, *Systematic Theology* (Grand Rapids: Eerdmans, 2010), 1:7.

2. Howard A. Snyder, "Wesley's Concept of the Church," *Asbury Seminarian* 33, no. 1 (1978): 38-40.

3. Geoffrey Wainwright, *Doxology: The Praise of God in Worship, Doctrine, and Life* (New York: Oxford University Press, 1980), 441.

Chapter 5

1. Franz Dünzl, *A Brief History of the Doctrine of the Trinity in the Early Church* (New York: T and T Clark, 2007).

2. Wainwright, *Doxology*, 180-81.

3. Robert Jenson, *Creed and Canon* (Louisville, KY: Westminster John Knox Press, 2010), 11-18.

4. George A. Lindbeck, *The Nature of Doctrine* (Louisville, KY: Westminster John Knox Press, 1984), 15-25.

5. Paul L. Holmer, *The Grammar of Faith* (New York: Harper and Row, 1978), 22, 25.

6. In what is known as the Definition of Faith of Chalcedon, the Council of Chalcedon (451) settled questions about the person of Christ. The Definition affirms one

person in two natures, "one and the same Christ, Son, Lord, only-begotten, acknowledged in two natures . . . each . . . being preserved . . . in one Person." For reasons too intricate to discuss here, strong minorities rejected the Definition.

7. The Athanasian Creed is also called the *Quicunque Vult*, Latin for the creed's first two words, "Whoever will be saved . . ." The first line continues, "before all things it is necessary that he hold the Catholic Faith." The creed is seldom used in Western Christianity. It is rejected by the Eastern Orthodox in part because it includes the *filioque* (v. 23), a phrase indicating the Holy Spirit proceeds from both the Father *and* the Son, rather than from the Father only.

8. Karl Barth, *Dogmatics in Outline* (New York: Harper and Row, 1959), 15-34.

9. *Book of Common Prayer*, 358.

10. "The Nicene Creed," *Sing to the Lord* (Kansas City: Lillenas, 1993), no. 14.

11. *Book of Common Prayer*, 358.

12. "Nicene Creed," *Sing to the Lord*, no. 14.

13. *Book of Common Prayer*, 359.

14. "Nicene Creed," *Sing to the Lord*, no. 14.

15. Wainwright, *Doxology*, 121-22.

16. Stephen G. Green, *The Holy Scriptures* (Kansas City: Foundry, 2021), 23-45, 163-82.

Chapter 6

1. Wainwright, *Doxology*, 354.

2. Ibid., 462.

3. Ibid., 8.

4. Ibid., 176.

5. Ibid., 8.

6. Ibid., 122.

7. Ibid., 183.

Chapter 7

1. Rob L. Staples, *Outward Sign and Inward Grace: The Place of Sacraments in Wesleyan Spirituality* (Kansas City: Beacon Hill Press of Kansas City, 1991), 22-25.

2. Staples proposes that the Wesleyan design of the sacraments should be seen as "spirit *via* structure." This is a powerful insight; there can be a both/and resolution. See *Outward Sign and Inward Grace*, 287.

3. Ibid., 22.

4. It should be noted that the denominations that still represent the holiness tradition do not agree on the sacraments. For example, the Salvation Army is nonsacramental (or omnisacramental, to be more precise), the Free Methodist Church affirms "real presence" explicitly, and the Wesleyan Church believes in believer's baptism only.

5. Robert Jenson, *Visible Words: The Interpretation and Practice of Christian Sacraments* (Minneapolis: Augsburg Fortress, 2010).

6. "Transubstantiation, Consubstantiation, or Something Else? Roman Catholic vs. Protestant Views of the Lord's Supper," adapted from Gregg R. Allison, *Historical Theology: An Introduction to Christian Theology* (Grand Rapids: Zondervan, 2011), *ZA Blog*, October 20, 2017, Zondervan Academic, https://zondervanacademic.com/blog/tran substantiation-consubstantiation-catholic-protestant.

7. Martin Luther, "Sermons on the Catechism, 1528: The Lord's Supper," *Martin Luther: Selections from His Writings*, ed. John Dillenberger (New York: Doubleday, 1961), 234-36; emphasis added.

8. "A Catechism," in *The Book of Common Prayer* (1662), maintained by Lynda M. Howell, http://www.eskimo.com/~lhowell/bcp1662/baptism/catchism.html.

9. "Of the Lord's Supper," art. 28 of Articles of Religion, in *The Book of Common Prayer* (1662; repr., London: John Baskerville, 1762), http://justus.anglican.org /resources/bcp/1662/articles.pdf.

10. Rob Staples offers a section on the theological meaning of Eucharist and Baptism. See *Outward Sign and Inward Grace*, ch. 5, "Baptism: Sacrament of Initiation," and ch. 7, "Eucharist: Sacrament of Sanctification."

11. In light of differences between holiness denominations, this chapter will be written from a Nazarene perspective (which has developed through the years).

12. "The Lord's Supper," *Manual, Church of the Nazarene, 2017–2021*, para., 13, p. 34.

13. *Book of Common Prayer*, 332.

14. Staples, *Outward Sign and Inward Grace*, 163-64.

15. See Al Truesdale, ed., *Square Peg: Why Wesleyans Aren't Fundamentalists* (Kansas City: Beacon Hill Press of Kansas City, 2012).

16. "By Water and the Spirit: A United Methodist Understanding of Baptism," A Report of the Baptism Study Committee, Dec. 19, 2008, United Methodist Church, https://www.umc.org/en/content/by-water-and-the-spirit-a-united-methodist-under standing-of-baptism.

Chapter 8

1. *Manual, Church of the Nazarene, 2017–2021*, para. 502.6.

2. Dallas Willard, *The Spirit of the Disciplines* (New York: HarperCollins, 1988), 184.

3. Henri Nouwen, *Spiritual Formation* (New York: HarperOne, 2010), 19.

4. Diane Leclerc and Mark Maddix, eds., *Spiritual Formation: A Wesleyan Paradigm* (Kansas City: Beacon Hill Press of Kansas City, 2011), 75.

5. Thomas C. Oden, *Pastoral Theology: Essentials of Ministry* (San Francisco: Harper and Row, 1983), 89.

6. Jeren Rowell, *Thinking, Listening, Being: A Wesleyan Pastoral Theology* (Kansas City: Beacon Hill Press of Kansas City, 2014), 70.

Chapter 9

1. On the role of Scripture in Christian ethics, Richard Hays observes that the task "must begin and end in the interpretation and application of Scripture for the life of the community." Richard B. Hays, *The Moral Vision of the New Testament* (San Francisco: HaperSanFrancisco, 1996), 10. See Hays's concise discussion of tradition, reason, and experience in relationship to the interpretation of Scripture (210-11).

2. The tendency to reduce Scripture to isolated passages necessitates a robust appreciation for the plenary nature of Scripture. As observed in the *Report of the Scripture Study Committee to the Twenty-Eighth General Assembly of the Church of the Nazarene*, "To say that the Bible *as a whole* is inspired is to say that we cannot take texts out of context and quote them arbitrarily as 'the word of God.' We have to understand biblical theology as a whole" (2), https://didache.nazarene.org/index.php/volume-13-1/892-didache-v13n1-01-scripturestudycommitteereport-king1/file.

3. Stanley Hauerwas and William H. Willimon, *Resident Aliens: Life in the Christian Colony* (Nashville: Abingdon Press, 1989), 85.

4. Ibid., 84. Addressing the task of Christian ethics, the writers state that "ethics is first a way of *seeing* before it is a matter of *doing*. The ethical task is not to tell you what is right or wrong but rather to train you to see" (95).

5. While one could argue that covenant is lacking in the biblical wisdom tradition, wisdom consistently insists that the "beginning of wisdom is the fear of Yhwh." Use of the name of the covenant God brings the biblical wisdom tradition fully within the range of covenant.

6. For a more extensive overview of the primary covenants in the biblical narrative, see Walter Brueggemann, *Reverberations of Faith: A Theological Handbook of Old Testament Themes* (Louisville, KY: Westminster John Knox Press, 2002), 37-40. See also Bill Arnold, "Covenant," in *Global Wesleyan Encyclopedia of Biblical Theology*, ed. Robert D. Branson (Kansas City: Foundry, 2020), 92-96.

7. Karl Barth rightly noted that while "creation is not itself the covenant," creation "prepares and establishes the sphere in which the institution and history of the covenant take place. Karl Barth, *Church Dogmatics,* III.1, ed. G. W. Bromiley and T. F. Torrance (London: T and T Clark International, 2004), 97.

8. Terence E. Fretheim, *God and World in the Old Testament: A Relational Theology of Creation* (Nashville: Abingdon Press, 2005), 19. Describing covenant as "the goal of creation," Barth comments that "the covenant whose history had still to commence was the covenant which, as the goal appointed for creation and the creature, made creation necessary and possible." Barth, *Church Dogmatics*, III.1, p. 231.

9. Barth, *Church Dogmatics*, III.1, p. 95.

10. Throughout this chapter, references to the *other* denote that which is distinct from the being of God.

11. Here we use Martin Buber's language of "I-Thou" and "I-It." Buber observed that "the world as experience belongs to the basic word I-It. The basic word I-You establishes the world of relation." Martin Buber, *I and Thou*, trans. Walter Kaufmann (New York: Touchstone, 1996), 56. He further noted that "when I confront a human being as my You and speak the basic word I-You to him, then he is no thing among things nor does he consist of things" (59).

12. See H. Ray Dunning's *Reflecting the Divine Image: Christian Ethics in Wesleyan Perspective* (Eugene, OR: Wipf and Stock, 2003), in which he explores the restoration of the divine image in humanity.

13. Fretheim, *God and World*, 19.

14. Walter Brueggemann, *Genesis*, Interpretation: A Bible Commentary for Teaching and Preaching (Louisville, KY: Westminster John Knox Press, 1982), 27.

15. Ibid., 154.

16. John Wesley, "The Preface," in *Hymns and Sacred Poems* (1739), viii, Duke Divinity School, https://divinity.duke.edu/sites/divinity.duke.edu/files/documents/cswt/04_Hymns_and_Sacred_Poems_%281739%29.pdf.

17. Perhaps the two New Testament words that approximate *hesed* are *agapē* (love) and *charis* (grace).

18. Bernhard W. Anderson, *Contours of Old Testament Theology* (Minneapolis: Fortress Press, 1999), 60.

19. John Wesley, *The Works of John Wesley*, 3rd ed. (Grand Rapids: Baker Books, 2002), 10:68.

Chapter 10

1. Dorothy Sayers, *Letters to a Diminished Church* (Nashville: W Publishing Group, 2004), 1.

2. Eugene H. Peterson, *Working the Angles: The Shape of Pastoral Integrity* (Grand Rapids: Eerdmans, 1987).

3. N. T. Wright, *Paul: A Biography* (New York: HarperOne, 2018), 384.

4. A revised version of Wesley's Covenant Renewal Service is made available by Discipleship Ministries of the United Methodist Church: https://www.umcdiscipleship.org/resources/covenant-renewal-service.

5. With predicates: "I am the bread of life" (John 6:35, 41, 48, 51, KJV); "I am the light of the world" (8:12, KJV); "I am the door of the sheep" (10:7, 9, KJV); "I am the resurrection, and the life" (11:25, KJV); "I am the good shepherd" (10:11, 14, KJV); "I am the way, the truth, and the life" (14:6, KJV); "I am the true vine" (15:1, 5, KJV).

6. Christ the King Sunday was instituted in 1925 by Pope Pius XI.

Chapter 11

1. Louisa M. R. Stead, "'Tis So Sweet to Trust in Jesus," in *Sing to the Lord*, no. 560.

2. Frederick W. Faber, "Faith of Our Fathers," in *Sing to the Lord*, no. 639.

3. Ray Palmer, "My Faith Looks Up to Thee," in *Sing to the Lord*, no. 433.

4. John R. W. Stott, *Your Mind Matters: The Place of the Mind in the Christian Life* (Downers Grove, IL: InterVarsity Press, 2006), 5.

5. Albert C. Outler theorized that Wesley used four different sources in coming to theological conclusions. Scripture was its foundation. However, doctrine had to be in keeping with Christian orthodox tradition. So tradition became in his view the second aspect of the so-called quadrilateral. Wesley believed that faith is more than merely an acknowledgment of ideas; as a practical theologian, he contended that part of the theological method would involve experiential faith. Finally, every doctrine must be able to be defended rationally. Tradition, experience, and reason, however, are subject always to Scripture, which is primary.

6. The means of grace are ways God works, sometimes invisibly, in Christians—"hastening, strengthening, and confirming faith so that God's grace pervades" all of life. The means of grace "can be divided into works of piety and works of mercy." United Methodist Communications, "The Wesleyan Means of Grace," United Methodist Church, https://www.umc.org/en/content/the-wesleyan-means-of-grace. This site also contains a detailed list of both kinds of means of grace.

7. This adapts Paul Tillich's "Method of Correlation," which correlates the questions implied in the situation with the answers implied in the message. It correlates human existence with divine manifestation.

8. Jaroslav Pelikan, interview by *U.S. News and World Report*, July 26, 1989, quoted by Scott Horton in "Pelikan on Tradition and Traditionalism." *Harper's Magazine*, December 27, 2008, https://harpers.org/2008/12/pelikan-on-tradition-and-traditionalism/.

9. Ibid.

10. Diane Leclerc, *Discovering Christian Holiness: The Heart of Wesleyan-Holiness Theology* (Kansas City: Beacon Hill Press of Kansas City, 2010), 271.

11. Ibid.

12. Stead, "'Tis So Sweet."

Chapter 12

1. Although Christians sometimes treat the terms "mission" and "missions" interchangeably, "missions" is best understood to refer to "the multitude of activities that God's people can engage in, by means of which they participate in God's mission." Christopher J. H. Wright, *The Mission of God's People: A Biblical Theology of the Church's Mission* (Grand Rapids: Zondervan, 2010), 25. "Missions," then, includes, but isn't limited to, cross-cultural ministry.

2. Dean Flemming, *Revelation and the Mission of God* (Downers Grove, IL: IVP Academic, forthcoming).

3. Wright, *Mission of God's People*, 73.

4. See Dean Flemming, *Why Mission?* (Nashville: Abingdon, 2015), 78-79.

5. See Michael J. Gorman, *Becoming the Gospel: Paul, Participation, and Mission* (Grand Rapids: Eerdmans, 2015).

6. Dean Flemming, "Mission," in *Dictionary of Paul and His Letters*, 2nd ed., ed. Scot McKnight, Lynn Cohick, and Nijay Gupta (Downers Grove, IL: IVP Academic, forthcoming).

7. For this section, see Ibid.

8. The Greek verb *epechō* can mean either "hold fast" or "hold forth" in Philippians 2:16 (I favor the latter). Either way, however, faithfulness to the gospel implies sharing the life-giving word when the opportunity arises.

9. H. Al Gilbert, "The Local Church and the Mission of God," in *Discovering the Mission of God: Best Missional Practices for the 21st Century*, ed. Mike Barnett and Robin Martin (Downers Grove, IL: IVP Academic, 2012), 600.

10. Gregg Okesson, *A Public Missiology: How Local Churches Witness to a Complex World* (Grand Rapids: Baker Academic, 2020).

11. Ibid., 219.

12. The Church in Action USA. https://www.churchinaction.com/.

13. Alan Kreider, *The Patient Ferment of the Early Church* (Grand Rapids: Baker Academic, 2016), 81.

BIBLIOGRAPHY

Barth, Karl. *Dogmatics in Outline*. New York: Harper and Row, 1959.

The Book of Common Prayer. New York: Seabury Press, 1979.

"By Water and the Spirit: A United Methodist Understanding of Baptism." A Report of the Baptism Study Committee, Dec. 19, 2008. United Methodist Church. https://www.umc.org/en/content/by-water-and-the-spirit-a-united-methodist-understanding-of-baptism.

"A Catechism." In *The Book of Common Prayer*. 1662. Maintained by Lynda M. Howell. http://www.eskimo.com/~lhowell/bcp1662/baptism/catchism.html.

The Church in Action USA. https://www.churchinaction.com/.

Crouch, Andy. *Culture Making: Recovering Our Creative Calling*. Downers Grove, IL: InterVarsity Press, 2013.

Delsol, Chantal. *Icarus Fallen*. Translated by Robin Dick. Wilmington, DE: ISI Books, 2003.

Dünzl, Franz. *A Brief History of the Doctrine of the Trinity in the Early Church*. New York: T and T Clark, 2007.

Flemming, Dean. "Mission." In *Dictionary of Paul and His Letters*. 2nd ed., edited by Scot McKnight, Lynn Cohick, and Nijay Gupta. Downers Grove, IL: IVP Academic, forthcoming.

———. *Revelation and the Mission of God*. Downers Grove, IL: IVP Academic, forthcoming.

———. *Why Mission?* Nashville: Abingdon, 2015.

Gilbert, H. Al. "The Local Church and the Mission of God." In *Discovering the Mission of God: Best Missional Practices for the 21st Century*, edited by Mike Barnett and Robin Martin, 600-609. Downers Grove, IL: IVP Academic, 2012.

Gorman, Michael J. *Becoming the Gospel: Paul, Participation, and Mission*. Grand Rapids: Eerdmans, 2015.

Green, Stephen G. *The Holy Scriptures*. Kansas City: Foundry, 2021.

Holmer, Paul L. *The Grammar of Faith*. New York: Harper and Row, 1978.

Jenson, Robert. *Creed and Canon*. Louisville, KY: Westminster John Knox Press, 2010.

———. *Visible Words: The Interpretation and Practice of Christian Sacraments*. Minneapolis: Augsburg Fortress, 2010.

Keller, Tim. "Tim Keller." In "Gospel Definitions," compiled by Trevin Wax. The Gospel Coalition. Updated September 2012. https://media.thegospel coalition.org/static-blogs/trevin-wax/files/2009/09/Gospel-Definitions .pdf.

Kreider, Alan. *The Patient Ferment of the Early Church*. Grand Rapids: Baker Academic, 2016.

Leclerc, Diane. *Discovering Christian Holiness: The Heart of Wesleyan-Holiness Theology*. Kansas City: Beacon Hill Press of Kansas City, 2010.

Leclerc, Diane, and Mark Maddix, eds. *Spiritual Formation: A Wesleyan Paradigm*. Kansas City: Beacon Hill Press of Kansas City, 2011.

Lindbeck, George A. *The Nature of Doctrine*. Louisville, KY: Westminster John Knox Press, 1984.

Luther, Martin. "Sermons on the Catechism, 1528: The Lord's Supper." *Martin Luther: Selections from His Writings*. Edited by John Dillenberger. New York: Doubleday, 1961.

Manual, Church of the Nazarene, 2017–2021. Kansas City: Nazarene Publishing House, 2017.

McKnight, Scot. "Kingdom Gospel 7." *Jesus Creed* (blog). Beliefnet.com. Accessed June 18, 2021. https://www.beliefnet.com/columnists/jesuscreed /2009/05/kingdom-gospel-7.html.

Nouwen, Henri. *Spiritual Formation*. New York: HarperOne, 2010.

Oden, Thomas C. *Pastoral Theology: Essentials of Ministry*. San Francisco: Harper and Row, 1983.

"Of the Lord's Supper." Art. 28 of Articles of Religion. In *The Book of Common Prayer*. 1662. Reprint, London: John Baskerville, 1762. http://justus.anglican .org/resources/bcp/1662/articles.pdf.

Okesson, Gregg. *A Public Missiology: How Local Churches Witness to a Complex World*. Grand Rapids: Baker Academic, 2020.

Pannenberg, Wolfhart. *Systematic Theology*. Vol. 1. Grand Rapids: Eerdmans, 2010.

Pelikan, Jaroslav. Interview by *U.S. News and World Report*, July 26, 1989. Quoted by Scott Horton in "Pelikan on Tradition and Traditionalism." *Harper's Magazine*, December 27, 2008. https://harpers.org/2008/12/pelikan -on-tradition-and-traditionalism/.

Peterson, Eugene H. *The Jesus Way: A Conversation on the Ways That Jesus Is the Way*. Grand Rapids: Eerdmans, 2007.

——. *Working the Angles: The Shape of Pastoral Integrity*. Grand Rapids: Eerdmans, 1987.

Piper, John, and N. T. Wright. "The Justification Debate: A Primer." *Christianity Today,* June 26, 2009.

Rowell, Jeren. *Thinking, Listening, Being: A Wesleyan Pastoral Theology*. Kansas City: Beacon Hill Press of Kansas City, 2014.

Sayers, Dorothy. *Letters to a Diminished Church*. Nashville: W Publishing Group, 2004.

Snyder, Howard A. "Wesley's Concept of the Church." *Asbury Seminarian* 33, no. 1 (1978): 38-40.

Staples, Rob L. *Outward Sign and Inward Grace: The Place of Sacraments in Wesleyan Spirituality*. Kansas City: Beacon Hill Press of Kansas City, 1991.

Stott, John R. *Your Mind Matters: The Place of the Mind in the Christian Life*. Downers Grove, IL: InterVarsity Press, 2006.

"Transubstantiation, Consubstantiation, or Something Else? Roman Catholic vs. Protestant Views of the Lord's Supper." Adapted from Gregg R. Allison. *Historical Theology: An Introduction to Christian Theology*. Grand Rapids: Zondervan, 2011. *ZA Blog*, October 20, 2017. Zondervan Academic, https://zondervanacademic.com/blog/transubstantiation-consubstantiation-catholic-protestant.

Truesdale, Al, ed. *Square Peg: Why Wesleyans Aren't Fundamentalists*. Kansas City: Beacon Hill Press of Kansas City, 2012.

United Methodist Communications. "The Wesleyan Means of Grace." United Methodist Church. https://www.umc.org/en/content/the-wesleyan-means-of-grace.

Wainwright, Geoffrey. *Doxology: The Praise of God in Worship, Doctrine, and Life*. New York: Oxford University Press, 1980.

Willard, Dallas. *The Spirit of the Disciplines*. New York: HarperCollins, 1988.

Wright, Christopher J. H. *The Mission of God's People: A Biblical Theology of the Church's Mission*. Grand Rapids: Zondervan, 2010.

Wright, N. T. *Paul: A Biography*. New York: HarperOne, 2018.

——. *Simply Good News: Why the Gospel Is News and What Makes It Good*. New York: HarperOne, 2015.